BｆT 5.77

SMALL-TOWN GIRL

SMALL-TOWN GIRL

Ellen Cooney

Houghton Mifflin Company   Boston   1983

J
C

Printed in the United States of America

V   10   9   8   7   6   5   4   3   2   1

Library of Congress Cataloging in Publication Data

Cooney, Ellen, 1948–
    Small-town girl.

    Summary: Colleen's relationship with her best friend,
her first love, her Catholic education, and her budding
literary talent are all vital parts of her life growing
up in a small Massachusetts town in the 1960s.
    [1. United States—Social life and customs—1945–
1970—Fiction.   2. Catholic schools—Fiction.   3. School
stories.   4. Friendship—Fiction]   I. Title.
PZ7.C7837Sm   1983   [Fic]   82–23379
ISBN 0–395–33881–6

To my parents, Vi and Will Cooney

 1961

Chapter one

The street where they lived began with the Protestant cemetery just outside the stooping brick rowhouses of the federal housing project. It rolled out beneath the old wooden railroad bridge, which hadn't been used for as long as anyone could remember. The bridge was decorated with spray-painted words Collie liked to mention now and then to get a rise out of her mother. Gathering steam for a quarter of a mile where front porches, their yellow eyes blinking, started tilting upward, the street careened up the steepest hill in town to the Catholic cemetery, where leafy paths were named for the passion and suffering of Jesus Christ.

There was usually a funeral coming or going. People of the street told the time of day by them. Housewives put down their dishcloths at the first sound of the hearse wheels and made their children hush. Old men sitting in the sun took off their hats. Jake Trombley, in his restaurant at the top of the hill, three doors up from the Dutton house, bowed his head respectfully whenever a funeral passed. Most of his business came from hungry mourners whose rattling stomachs weren't used to having breakfast in the middle of the day.

Arthur Bent took his coffee at Jake's Grille every morning. Most days he sat at the window with a perfect view of the ten-foot-high crucifix that marked the resting place of the monsignor who had built the Catholic church. The crucifix was a simple gray stone, unadorned, rising out of a geranium mound that seemed to bloom all year long. Arthur Bent's contracting company had made that crucifix with its own cement and had given it to the church for free. But today Arthur Bent sat at Jake's counter, quietly stirring his spoon round and round in his empty cup.

"Got something on your mind, Art?" said Jake, wiping a dish.

Arthur Bent looked over his shoulder at the girl huddled at a table overlooking Agony in the Garden Avenue, where yawning caretakers were laying planks over the hole they had just dug. Now and then she would turn to the window indifferently, vacantly, as if she were staring out at some mysterious thing in the landscape invisible to everyone else. A book lay open before her on the table.

"Out with it, Art. Ain't nobody here but you and me and Clarey Dutton's oldest girl. Got her nose so far in that book o' hers she don't even know what planet she's on."

Arthur Bent held out his coffee mug for a refill. Stirring in a lump of sugar, he leaned forward on the countertop and answered softly, "I'm goin' to do it, Jake. I been thinkin' and thinkin' on it, and I'm goin' to do it."

"Yeah, Art?"

"That's right, Jake."

There was a long, heavy pause.

"Do what, Art?"

Arthur Bent laid down his spoon. Like a secret agent delivering a deadly code word to a man on a stool in a tiny windowless room, one finger poised at the end of a button, he said, "I'm goin' to renovate my cellar."

Collie Dutton looked up as though she'd been struck. The shock of Mr. Bent's admission sent chills running thrillingly right through her. It was almost too much to bear.

Mr. Bent was going to renovate his cellar.

Renovate his cellar!

So that was it.

So that was why Ruthanne Bent had said yesterday at civil defense drill that she would never have to spend a night in any smelly damp church basement and drink holy water once the dam was contaminated after the bombs hit.

So that was it.

And to think I called her a prissface! thought Collie, leaping into her coat.

"Get on there, girl! It's five minutes till the bell rings," called Jake. "That mother o' yours ever finds out I let you in here mornings to read, she'll have my can in a sling. Girls your age ought to be outdoors gettin' exercise an' sun. Off with you now!" Jake turned back to his customer. "You know, Art, you might consider tellin' folks you're buildin' a swimmin' pool and keep the thing inside a fence. Camouflage it, so to speak. Otherwise you'll have half the town at your doorstep the minute it, God forbid, ever happens. Least that's what I did."

"Naw," said Arthur Bent. "I already got a swimmin' pool. Cellar renovations is what I'm callin' it. Cellar renovations'll have to do."

Heart thumping wildly, Collie flew out the door.

During penmanship class Sister Mary Grace, writing on the blackboard, turned on her radar in time to catch the ripple of the note being passed hand under desk, hand under desk, hand under desk to Ruthanne Bent. She was not fast enough to catch the note itself. It said:

> I don't really think you're a prissface and I
> don't blame you if you never speak to me
> again. I'm sorry if I hurt your feelings.
> I was in a terrible mood and took it out on
> you. Yours extremely truly, your friend
> (I hope) Colleen.

"Miss Dutton? Miss Dutton, have you something to say?" Sister Mary Grace didn't turn her head. Her hand remained on the blackboard.

"No, Sister."

"Perhaps you might speak for yourself to the entire class. Come down here, young lady."

Behind two hands cupped for a series of noisy sneezes in case she was found out, Ruthanne read the note. After a very long moment, during which Collie felt as if her very life were being judged and found worthless, Ruthanne looked up and smiled. From the front of the class Collie watched her writing her reply.

> I forgive you because I didn't think
> you really meant it. It was mean of Sister
> to make you stand in front of the class
> all morning. Your friend, Ruthie.

Collie flashed Ruthanne a grin. Her bright eyes reminded Collie of a goldfish in a bowl. They weren't so bad once you got used to them. They were sort of pretty—deep-set and shimmery—even if they did go off at opposite angles. Perhaps she was able to see more that way.

"Do you know what the Communists have done in the last forty-five years?" asked the phonograph record in Sister Mary Edwina's social studies class that afternoon. "In forty-five years the Communist regime, that octopus lunging at the free world with its demonic tentacles of intrigue, false propaganda, and brute military force, has swallowed up one-fourth of the earth's surface and consumed in its vicious gulp over one billion people!"

The needle pricked its way forward scratchily, allowing the sixth grade a moment to register the information.

"And do you think this beast will be satisfied with consuming small fishes, with tiny poor countries on the other side of the world that are barely able to scratch a living off their rocky soil? No! Certainly not! At this very minute the odious Red Menace is plotting to grind away at the very

5

foundations of our great Democracy, to destroy you and me and the government laid down by the sweat and blood of our illustrious forefathers, to replace our President with an alien of the U.S.S.R.!"

Scratch, scratch, went the needle. Collie eyed Ruthanne hopefully. For months she had been begging her father, then her mother, then her father and mother together, to build the only thing in the world they truly needed for survival, a bomb shelter. Her father had called it her over-active imagination. Her mother had called it a waste of money. "We'll go when the Lord calls us and not a moment before," her mother had said. Ruthanne Bent was her only hope.

"Listen, boys and girls," came the recording as a tinny marching band struck up a lively rhythm. A chorus of children with husky, strangely clipped voices sang out noisily in a foreign language. Collie found her feet swinging to the beat below her desk. Ashamed, she clamped her hands to her knees.

"Those children you heard are the children who are this very moment being trained at propaganda schools. Do not be deceived by their false cheer. One day those children may be the very ones who . . ."

Press the button! thought Collie with the usual sinking feeling, imagining a horror worse than the pictures of mushroom clouds floating over Hiroshima, worse than the Safety Week films of bodies sizzling by the wrecks of cars that jammed too late to avoid hitting a child running after her ball in the road—worse than all that, this final devastating explosion that would happen out of her hearing but would poison all the water, all the cows, all the gardens, and kill the people slowly, one by one. No matter what her parents said, the bomb was going to come. Most of the time she did not think much about anything else.

". . . press the button," scratched the needle. "And you all know what will happen then."

Every head in the classroom bobbed knowingly as the record screeched to a stop.

It was over. Sister Mary Edwina, who always lowered the shades and shut off the lights for auditory lessons, opened them. Collie rubbed her eyes and wrote a note reminding Ruthanne to sit next to her at lunch.

Chapter two

 "Dead souls live in these trees," Collie said.
Ruthanne's expression went from blank
disbelief to plain terror as she looked upward. One of her
eyes stole cautiously toward her left ear. The other one was
having a hard time lifting itself from the bridge of her
nose.

"They go there for shelter. You know, the souls of people who were buried with unfinished business. Most of
them died when they didn't expect to, or else they were
having an argument with somebody and didn't finish it."

Ruthanne shivered, her eyes two clear, unblinking circles
of fright.

"Sometimes I come up here at night to listen for the
souls. But mostly all I hear is the trees creaking. I mean, I
suppose it's the trees creaking. You wouldn't expect a soul
to *creak*, would you?"

They were sitting cross-legged in the circle of pine trees
that intersected Jesus Is Nailed to the Cross and Scourging

at the Pillar lanes. The dim, shadowy enclosure was originally meant for private prayer services following the funerals of especially prominent members of the parish, but the church hardly ever used it. Collie used it all the time. She kept her father's World War II mess kit, an old deflated rubber raft for damp days, and a flashlight stored away in the branches of a pine tree she had named Madame, to which she directed the most dramatic of her poems.

> *You may think pine trees are boring,*
> *For their colors remain the same.*
> *But think of ships in a mooring,*
> *Remaining the way that they came.*
> *A pine tree doesn't need seasons,*
> *To tell her the way she must dress.*
> *And I don't need any reasons,*
> *To know when I like a thing best.*

"There, do you see any souls?"

Collie aimed the flashlight over the quivering, droopy branches. She thought it was most unbecoming of Ruthanne to dribble crumbs from her sandwich all over her chin, but she thoughtfully didn't mention it. With a tumultuous roll Ruthanne's eyes took in everything, the thick gnarled roots representing the face of Jesus receiving forty lashes on His back, Collie's knees, the peanut butter jar they had stuck in Madame's branches to keep the ants away, and the mighty grace of the fir trees reaching upward, their arms bowing heavily under the weight of the souls.

Ruthanne bit her lips in awe.

9

"You're not scared, are you?"

Ruthanne shook her head.

"Good. It's silly to be scared about death. Did you know the only true fact of life besides the fact that we were born is that we are going to die?"

Ruthanne nodded seriously.

"Don't you think that's terribly sad?"

Ruthanne looked down. "I suppose you're right. All the same, I happen to know that I'm going to die of natural causes. And not until I'm old. Real, real old. Older than even Mrs. Tartaglia."

Mrs. Tartaglia was the Duttons' next-door neighbor. She had been old for as long as anyone could remember. The times she showed herself on her back porch or struggling down the steps to the bird-feeder in her back yard, there seemed to be nothing to her but a series of points trying their best to connect. Her clothes flapped senselessly around her clothesline-pole-thin body. Collie wanted to pick up Mrs. Tartaglia and carry her every time she saw her trying to walk. Mrs. Tartaglia's big dark eyes said, over and over, everything hurts, everything hurts.

Collie jerked the flashlight beam toward Ruthanne's look of smug self-righteousness. Disembodied, her face seemed to float slowly among the boughs. It gave Collie the creeps, and she snapped off the light.

"How do you know that, Ruthie? How do you know you're going to die of natural causes?"

"Is that all you can think about? Death?"

"Of course not. I just want to know how you know."

It was time for Ruthanne to say: *I know because my*

father is having our cellar renovated. Silently, Collie urged
her on.

But Ruthanne only said it was time to change the subject.

Mrs. Tartaglia died. Collie wondered why Angela
Tartaglia, a twelfth-grader who wore lipstick and liked
boys to carry her books home from school, should get a
week off from school just because her grandmother died.
Black awnings went up over the Tartaglia windows, and a
black wreath covered the back door. It was impossible to
see inside. What was Angela Tartaglia doing in there?
Probably painting her fingernails and gobbling up fruit-
cakes, that's what.

"The girl's in mourning," cried Clare Dutton, appalled.
"Angela Tartaglia is mourning the death of her grandmother, who loved her. You are without a doubt the most
insensitive girl I know, Colleen. Imagine! You of all people!"

Shoving her hands in her pockets, Collie threw her
mother a look of quick, cold anger and rushed away.

Mrs. Tartaglia lay in a funeral home in an enormous
metal coffin. Her hands looked as if they'd been borrowed
from a department store mannequin. They were folded
across her chest. In the awful stillness of death she had
somehow put on weight, gained a complexion that was
flushed a queer shade of scarlet. None of it had anything to
do with Mrs. Tartaglia.

Collie breathed a prayer that when the bomb came she would be among the first to be killed.

"Spare me, O Lord, from malingering," she whispered.

"Go ahead and kiss her goodbye," said Clare from the foot of the coffin. "Show your respect."

Collie's younger sister, Mary, tall and bony and looking very uncomfortable in her best dress, obediently stood on tiptoe and pressed her lips against the sickeningly surd cheek. When Mary looked up, there were on her mouth unmistakable traces of white powder, pieces of the decomposition of Mrs. Tartaglia. When Collie's turn could not go untaken she carefully kissed the satin edges of the pillow supporting the dead head so it wouldn't fall off.

In the car on the way home from the wake, Clare and Mary wept openly. Collie asked if they could stop for ice cream, and Clare burst into a new round of tears.

"When your Nana died, God rest her soul, Daddy and I didn't bring you along to wake her. And thank the Lord for that! You were only eight years old, Colleen, but you were just as heartless at eight as you are now. It would have broken your Nana's heart to know what a heartless girl you are! Especially you being right there when we lost her. Hmmf! I suppose you'd like to see me dead so you can have a month off from school. I suppose if your father and I were to die tomorrow in a car crash, God forbid, you'd give a party!"

To soothe her, Collie wrote a poem:

My, how the tears flowed in rivers
When my parents were laid in their grave,
But all I showed were my shivers,
For I knew they'd like me to be brave.

From north and south and east and west,
People wished that my parents weren't dead.
But I, the one who loved them best,
Did my crying inside of my head.

"Every time you write us a poem, we're dead," sniffed Clare. "Now why can't you sit down and write about something happy, like my lilies blooming away in December? How many people in Currys Crossing have a lily plant that blooms in the middle of winter?"

Martin Dutton, listening nearby, pointed out that they really shouldn't take it too personally: in Collie's poems everybody was dead.

Clare hoped it was just a phase.

The newspapers were screaming about Russia's plans to invade United States–held territory somewhere in the Atlantic Ocean. Looking over her father's shoulder at the headlines, Collie figured out that the island under Russian consideration lay not more than one hundred miles to the east of Massachusetts. It would take a bomb less than ninety seconds to reach her own home.

But nobody seemed worried. Why?

*   *   *

Collie scooped up a handful of earth and stuck her flashlight, beam upward, in the ground. "Remember, Ruthie, this is a candle."

"Okay."

"You ever do this before?"

"Nope."

"Not with anyone?"

"Nope. You?"

"Of course not. I said you were the first."

Collie took a deep, dramatic breath and twirled herself around until the trees merged one into the other, a swimming circle of green. Placing her right hand over her heart, she faced the monsignor's crucifix and shut her eyes. "I, Colleen Dutton, do here swear to be best friend to Ruthanne Bent. I promise to stick by her, to protect her name and her person, and to do things she likes, even if I hate them, for as long as we both shall live, amen."

Collie bowed her head as Ruthanne took her turn. She'd never noticed before how Ruthanne's strawberry hair caught pieces of sunlight like a prism. How melodic her voice was, how soft, how calm! How the minuscule freckles on her face and arms caught the eye, their intricate patterns signifying something whose meaning was yet to be discovered. Ruthanne looked at Collie and smiled shyly. The corners of her mouth darted into infinitely interesting dimples.

They sat crosslegged on the ground staring into the candle till their eyes ached.

"I, Colleen Dutton, do here pledge the blood of my life as a symbol of the best friend I have this day pledged myself to in the hopes that this sacrifice may be acceptable to her for the praise and honor of our friendship. I offer this my blood in a humble spirit and contrite heart and pray she may find it wholly pleasing in every way, amen."

The safety pin that had been holding a pocket to Collie's skirt flashed in a sunbeam.

"I, Ruthanne Bent, do here pledge the blood of my life as a symbol of . . ."

Gulping, Collie stuck out her index finger, gritted her teeth, and plunged in the pin. Quickly she passed it to Ruthanne. They pressed their fingers together. They counted ten.

"Okay," said Collie eagerly. "Now we have to tell a secret."

Chapter three

 In Sister Mary Rose of Lima's science class a note was passed hand under desk, hand under desk, hand under desk to Ruthanne Bent.

Dear Ruthie, About that matter we discussed: I will never, never, ever tell anyone about your B__b S_____r. Because you told me, and asked your father if I could come along when It happens, means you are truly my best friend. The very best. About that thing I told you. Everyone thinks my aunt Juney was in the hospital having her appendix out. If my mother ever found out I told you what really happened she would kill me. I'm not even supposed to know about it because when the ambulance came and took her away they thought I was at girl scouts, but I already quit and didn't tell them yet. I won't even tell my sister Mary about the B__b S_____r, but do you think when It happens she could come too? She's a good kid. You said you wish you had a sister. Maybe we could share her. I'm not worried about my parents because they'll probably be dead by then. Your Friend, Colleen.

The reply came at lunch:

Dear Colleen, my very truest of friends, Let's not tell my father about Mary coming along but sneak her in, okay? For the first few months we can hide her under a mattress, then let her out like we didn't know she was there. I promise honestly never to tell anyone in the universe about your aunt June's N_____s B_____n but one time I heard my mother say she heard that your aunt was having problems coping. Even if she asks me though I'll say I don't know, or that it was her appendix. I can't write anymore. Sister Mary Lima Bean is eyeballing me. From your Friend, Ruthie.

Dear Ruthie, in answer to your question a vertebrate is anything with a backbone. Just remember if you step on something and it squishes without crunching it's not a vertebrate. A worm is not. A frog is.

Dear Colleen, I never told anybody this but you said we had to tell everything. Once when I was riding my bike I ran (accidentally) over a baby squirrel. It crunched all right. First I felt the crunch right underneath my foot then I heard it. Wouldn't you think it'd be the other way round? There wasn't any blood, it just lay there with its head flattened. I would've buried it but just when I was getting off my bike a whole bunch of squirrels appeared and I thought they might bite me. You know how squirrels can be. Anyway it happened a long time ago. When I was eight. But I never forgot that crunch.

Dear Ruthie, That's the most disgusting thing I ever

heard of, but know what I did once? I was real little, about five, and my sister was a baby. She still had her soft spot. You know, the one in the middle of the head. I used to press it to see what would happen. I thought my finger might poke through so I could see what a brain felt like. But it just bounced back. Too bad squirrels' heads weren't like that or that baby you murdered would still be alive.

Dear Colleen, I did not murder it. It was an accident. What about the time you sprayed your mother's tulips with the rug cleaner and they shriveled?

Dear Ruthie, That was an accident. I thought it was bug spray.

Dear Colleen, You did not.

Dear Ruthie, I did too.

Dear Colleen, You did not. You hated those tulips.

Dear Ruthie, I don't want to talk about it anymore and if you do go find somebody else to talk to.

Dear Colleen, Maybe I will.

Dear Ruthie, Thank you for taking me down to your B__b S_____r. It wasn't what I expected. I expected something like a cave, cool and damp, maybe fixed up with a rug and some pillows, and of course oxygen tanks. But was I surprised when it was a regular room! I like the way your mother fixed the bunkbeds against the wall and all the pretty curtains and pictures. If I were you I'd start living there right now. Let's go down there after school for homework. Nobody will know, and we'll use the secret entrance. Did you understand what Sister said about the Bomb? Probably she meant it will land in Washington

D.C., on the White House, so we won't have to worry about that, and before Fallout starts we'll have time to pack a suitcase and get to the B__b S_____r. I'm worried about two things: (1) That we won't be able to find my sister when It happens and I promised on my honor that I wouldn't tell her ahead of time about your B__b S_____r. (2) What if the Russians press their Button first? My father says in that case we have radar that will automatically set off the sirens, but I know my father and he has an explanation for everything because he doesn't believe in worrying. The encyclopedia says the H-Bomb can't be detected till it's too late, and what if Fallout already starts while we're in school, or on the way there? By the time we get to the B__b S_____r we may be dying of leukemia. Then what? It's incurable. It's a disease of the blood cells, and first your hair falls out, then your skin. It's very painful. I'd rather be in Washington D.C. and have the Bomb land on me and get it over with. How about you?

Dear Colleen, My father says we have spies in Moscow who will telephone the President on the Hot Line the second the Reds push the Button. That way we'll have plenty of time to get to the B__b S_____r because the sirens will go off. We've practiced it so often that we'll know exactly what to do. About Mary: let's tell her to meet us at Jake's Grille (or just you so she doesn't suspect). Okay?

Dear Ruthie, Okay. I finished the answers to the questions at the end of chapter eight and wrote you a poem. Tell me if you like it.

The way raindrops tap a leaf,
Bending, bending, bending;
The way gardeners touch a sheaf,
Tending, tending, tending;
The way a nun fasts in Lent,
Mending, mending, mending;
Are the ways of Ruthanne Bent,
Friending, friending, friending.

Dear Colleen, It's beautiful, much nicer than the poems in our books, which are mushy and childish. Let's send it to the Poetry Corner of the *Clarion*. My father knows the Editor and it'll be sure to get in. Okay?

Dear Ruthie, No, no, no, no, no! A thousand times no! That's *personal*.

Dear Colleen, They pay five dollars. Please?

Dear Ruthie, No. If you do without telling me I'll never speak to you again as long as we both shall live and you can get some other girl to go to your B__b S_____r. I'll just crawl under a rock and get radiated.

Dear Colleen, Well you don't have to get so mad. I'd rather get radiated with you than go to the B__b S_____r without you. Love, Ruthie.

AHrrrr-AWK!
AHrrrr-AWK!
AHrrrr-AWK! came the piercing wail of the alarm. The children dropped their pencils and waited at their desks to see if it meant a fire or a bomb drill, to see if they should

simply file out to the schoolyard or cover their faces and run in a calm orderly manner to the church basement.

AHrrrr-AWK! AHRA AHRA RAWK!

AHrrrr-AWK! AHRA AHRA RAWK!

AHRRRR-AWK! AHRA AHRA RAWK!

Bombs. Every time there was a drill Collie thought, Is this it? She wondered while they scurried into line, smallest ones first, taking care not to breathe, if she'd ever see her mother again, what it felt like to die, what they'd get to eat in the long years it took to decontaminate the air, the water, the farms.

"Hurry, children!" called the nuns, veils over their mouths. They looked like bashful sea animals. Their skirts flapped as they strode through the yard. Now and then a nun swooped down to carry a lagging first-grader or to remove a slingshot from a boy's hand.

AHRRRR-AWK! AHRA AHRA RAWK! screeched the signal after them, though she dared not look back. She imagined a stupendous mushroom cloud forming over their country, racing toward them on swift, omnipotent wings.

"Aren't you glad we don't have to stay in any smelly damp basement?" whispered Ruthanne as the girls took their places on the floor where the church's Nativity crèche was stored.

"Now, children, lie down," boomed Mother Superior through a megaphone. "Flat on the floor with your hands over your ears. Everyone remain calm and lie quietly."

The youngest ones giggled as their bodies touched the cool cement. Someone knocked over a cardboard box and three Wise Men tumbled out. A little girl cried for her mother.

"Quiet, children, quiet down. Is everyone lying still now? Girls—girls, I said we must all lie down flat!"

"Don't do it," whispered Collie. "The boys look up your skirts."

"You two girls, lie down or else take your place with Sister Mary Benedictine's kindergarten!"

"We better do it," answered Ruthanne. "Hold your knees together real tight and cross your ankles all the way round, and they won't see a thing."

"I hope they go cross-eyed trying," muttered Collie, pressing herself to the floor.

Dear Ruthie, The most amazing thing! I just finished reading this book and did you know that Russia used to have emperors and courts and princesses before the Communists came? There was a revolution and everyone died. Tonight hurry up and get your geography done and I'll come to the B__b S_____r to tell you about it. Wait till you see these pictures! The princesses are beautiful.

Dear Colleen, How can you say a Russian is beautiful?

Dear Ruthanne, Just wait till you see these princesses. They played with emeralds and rode dogsleds and slept on blankets made of fur. Wait till you see their Easter baskets!

Dear Colleen, I don't think I can look at them.

Dear Ruthie, Why not? You're the one who likes princesses.

Dear Colleen, Not Russian ones.

Dear Ruthie, Well you don't have to be so picky. Anyway they're only pictures.

Dear Colleen, I wasn't going to tell you this but you said we have to tell everything so meet me at the Pines after school.

Dear Ruthie, Tell me now.

Dear Colleen, Meet me at the Pines, okay?

Ruthie, If you don't tell me right this minute I'll tell everyone in this classroom you have a B__b S_____r. Then you'll get it!

Dear Colleen, If you insist. My father said he saw you at Jake's with a book by a Russian.

Ruthie, That's what I'm talking about. The book about the emperor and everything.

Dear Colleen, My father said it was a Communist book.

Ruthie, Don't be an idiot. I got it from my father.

Dear Colleen, Well that's what I mean.

Dear Ruthie, What do you mean exactly?

Dear Colleen, My father said your mother's the only one of the people he went to school with who married somebody from out of town. I forget where your father's from. I told my father I thought California but he said nobody can be sure.

Ruthie! Of course my father's from California. Where do you think I got my Golden Gate Bridge locket from, Siberia?

Dear Colleen, My father said that your father goes to secret meetings every week.

Dear Ruthie, He does not.

Dear Colleen, Yes he did. My father doesn't lie. Where does your father go on Tuesday nights?

Dear Ruthie, None of your business, Prissface.

Dear Colleen, Well if that's the way you're going to be about it my father said I can't be best friends with you anymore because your father is a C_____t.

Dear Ruthie, My father is NOT A COMMUNIST.

Dear Colleen, My father DOESN'T LIE.

Dear Ruthie, I'LL NEVER GO INTO YOUR STINKY BOMB SHELTER AGAIN PRISSFACE FISH EYES. I HOPE RADIATION ROTS YOUR HEART OUT. YOU MAKE ME SICK. Your ex-friend, Colleen. P.S. I'll cut off the finger your blood touched before I ever look at you again. And don't write me another note because I won't read it. I'll spit on it and stamp it to dust.

Clare was on her hands and knees, scraping frost off shelves in the icebox when Collie stormed in, banging things.

"Where does Daddy go on Tuesday nights?"

Clare answered over her shoulder, "You know where, Colleen. To the city to teach his class. Hand me a towel, will you?"

"How do you know that?"

"What do you mean, how do I know that? Of course I know that. Daddy's been doing it for years. Will you hand me a towel?"

Collie flung a dishcloth at her mother. Her chest was heaving rapidly, her hands two fists looking for something to pound. "What if he was going somewhere else, how would you know?"

"Because he's your father and he'd tell me. Smell this milk. I think it's gone sour."

Collie stamped her foot. "Can you prove it?"

"For heaven's sake, Colleen, prove what?"

"That he goes where he says he goes."

"Colleen, I've got work to do. Does the milk seem bad?"

"Smell it yourself. I can't tell."

She stole quietly into her father's room, looking for something on his desk.

There it was: Accounting 203, Martin F. Dutton, Tuesday, 7:00 to 9:30. Collie sat on her father's chair. Hot stinging tears filled her eyes. She pounded the desk till her hands hurt, pretending it was Ruthanne Bent's stupid dull treacherous face. The following morning Jake Trombley asked her not to come to his restaurant to read anymore because it was bothering the customers.

"What happened to Ruthie Bent? I thought you two were best friends," said Clare.

"Who's Ruthie Bent? I never heard of any Ruthie Bent."

"Oh, come on now, darling. If you two quarreled, then make it up. Everyone has to have a friend."

"What for? All I'm going to do anyway is die. Who needs friends when they're dead?"

> *Why should sparrows gather crumbs,*
> *When it's too cold to fly?*
> *Why should squirrels store their nuts,*
> *When all they can do is die?*
> *The thing to be is an angel,*

With radiant wings to spread.
Because at least when you're an angel,
You're safe and already dead.

Over his newspaper Martin Dutton said that the politicians running the United States of America were a bunch of mules. Why didn't someone kick the asses where—

"Oh, Daddy!" cried Collie in tears. "Do you have to say things like that?" Pushing herself away from the table, she spilled milk into her sister's soup and fled to her room.

"I just don't know what's got into her lately," sighed Clare.

 1962

Chapter four

It was almost spring. Between cemeteries, windows were flung open and neighbors greeted each other enthusiastically, sniffing the air like rabbits. Though melted snow ran everywhere, the children left their boots in school and went home through puddles, coats flapping round their shoulders. Jake Trombley put a "Closed for Vacation" sign in his window and went up north to fish. Mrs. Arthur Bent covered the false windows of the family bomb shelter with pretty new gingham curtains and put the pillows out for an airing. On Jesus Carries His Cross Avenue lilac buds reappeared along with the cracked headstones of women who had led remarkably brief lives. Flags at veterans' graves defrosted and billowed in the slow smooth wind. Within the circle of pines the ground oozed thickly, and Collie had to fold her rubber mat in half in order to sit there comfortably while recording plenary indulgences in the prayer diary she'd started that winter. It was her hope to spend as little time as possible in the fires of purgatory.

Her notebook was filled with names of prayers arranged by the length of time each one gained. Beside them were dates and totals. December had been a productive month: thanks to strict Advent observance she'd run up two hundred eighty-three years. January had slackened, but in February she'd faithfully said the Litany of the Sacred Heart of Jesus on her way to school as she walked alone; and on the way home, alone, said the Litany to the Most Holy Virgin, hoping that the way her feet touched the ground with a mystical rose, tower of David; a morning star, gate of heaven; a spiritual vessel, vessel of honor, singular vessel of devotion, pray pray pray for me, would somehow make the hurt a little less painful. This way she bought herself fourteen years of grace each day. The hurt stayed.

She threw back her head and watched the dripping pine trees, imagining in their boughs the white shimmering face of the Most Holy Virgin as She had appeared to the children of Fatima. Oh why don't You appear to me, thought Collie. Then maybe Ruthanne might like me again.

The pines swayed back and forth, back and forth. Remembering her purpose, Collie gathered herself to pray the Purgatory Prayer. She closed her eyes.

> *Out of the depths I cry to You,*
> *O Lord,*
> *Lord hear my voice!*
> *Let Thine Ear be attentive to my supplications!*

Calm and lighthearted, for not only had she just received another seven years of freedom from punishment, but a suffering soul was, thanks to her, just lifted out of the Fires, she shook one of Madame's branches and sent sweet drops falling all over her mouth. She licked them away and went on with her real business, a plan that was so secret she dared not commit it to paper.

Wasn't a sin not really a sin if the sinner repented beforehand?

Or was a sin a sin at all if accomplished not out of real evil but out of necessity?

What Arthur Bent had done was evil; perhaps not the evil that creeps into the look of a man with a finger at the trigger of a gun, but evil all the same. Lying, slander, defamation of character, cruel and malicious intent to ruin the name of a good man by telling the whole town he was not a good man at all but the very worst thing one could say of anyone—no, there seemed no way round what Mr. Bent had done. He had called her father a Communist. That made her the daughter of one. If it wasn't a mortal sin, she decided, it ought to be. It was a thing that must be atoned for.

Looking at the newspaper later that day, she was mortified: a photograph of a Negro girl, schoolbag in hand, her face a grim contorted mask of pain and hard bewildered fear, assaulted from all sides by rock-throwing, jeering children and grownups. All of them were bigger than the girl, and whiter. Collie looked at the picture for a long time.

"Them coloreds," said the mailman. "Why can't they go back where they came from and leave well enough alone?"

"Next thing you know," said men smoking cigars on their front porches, "schools we pay our money on'll be run right to hell."

Ruthanne Bent, who looked the other way every time Collie passed, said her father would allow a colored man in their house as long as she was away or locked in her room with her mother.

"The Russians pay Negroes to start trouble," said Ruthanne loudly. "It's a plot to weaken our nation from within."

Collie, who had never seen a Negro except in books and movies, forsook her own indulgences to pray that one day the little girl in the newspaper picture would come to her school. She was certain the little girl was her age, twelve, and would be a good friend, would never stab her in the back by calling her father a Communist. Collie pretended the girl's family moved next door, as the men said Negroes would. She named the girl Amanda and decided Amanda loved reading, scraping off pine bark to get at the sap, and Collie. They would do everything together, proving to the whole town the power of friendship. The newspaper would run a story:

LOCAL GIRLS CROSS RACE BARRIER
Children Say: Coloreds and Whites Live in Peace

Because his daughter was a hero, Martin Dutton would never again be whispered about. Together, Collie and Amanda would build their own bomb shelter and invite their families. Together, they would bring about the ruin of Arthur Bent.

At the all-school assembly on Brotherly Love Day, Collie stood on the stage to read the poem she'd written for the occasion:

> *What if I woke up one morning*
> *With my skin turned chocolate brown,*
> *Would you call me names and hit me,*
> *And chase me far from your town?*
> *Is not a Negro a person,*
> *Who like us comes from a seed?*
> *If you tell a joke won't she laugh?*
> *If you prick her won't she bleed?*
> *We aren't a single bit better,*
> *Just because we were born white.*
> *God wants us to love the Negroes,*
> *As the daytime must love the night.*

The nuns gave her a heart-shaped award for excellence in English but no Negro children came to town. Several Puerto Rican families moved in though, and set up house in the federal project. Soon all the white people living there moved away. The men said those spicks (pulling back their lips, wrinkling their noses as though swallowing something foul, they said those *spicks*) those spicks won't last a winter. But soon the project was full of the bronze-skinned, fast-talking, thin wiry children who could outrun anyone daring enough to race them. They had their own school in one of the apartments. The priests said Mass in Spanish Sunday afternoons in the church basement. The civil defense stopped cleaning out the project shelter after all-town drills. Collie and her sister were ordered to stop riding bikes through the Protestant cemetery. Jake Trombley's cousin Bill, who though a Catholic was the Protestants' caretaker, said he'd take his strap to any town kid he caught there. And if for some reason it was necessary for a girl to walk by the project, it must be in daylight and always accompanied by a parent or a boy. Ruthanne Bent told everyone at school that the Puerto Ricans kidnapped white girls and sold them to the Russians to have money for big expensive American cars. It was reverse slavery, said Ruthanne. It was a plot to weaken our nation from within. Looking at Collie she said: You know all about things like that, don't you, Colleen?

Chapter five

Collie couldn't remember the name of the movie whose plot she was stealing from, but she remembered the important parts. Bette Davis had a sinister younger brother who drank too much and was insanely jealous of the Bulgarian count Bette Davis was about to marry. Because the brother had vowed to do anything in the world to prevent the wedding ceremony, he had to be temporarily shut up. Bette Davis put something into his martini on her wedding day, and he was out cold for hours. The climax of the movie came when Bette Davis, still in her wedding gown, sat anxiously by her brother's bedside, praying he wasn't going to die. He didn't. But the movie never made clear exactly what she put into his drink or how much. Collie had puzzled over it for weeks. She did not want Mr. Bent to die. She did not want Mr. Bent out cold. All she wanted to do was show people that Mr. Bent was not exactly the person everyone thought him to be. She chose the night of her class's Confirmation, when girls secretly cringing inside the unfamiliar press of garter belts holding up their first nylon stockings, and necktied boys in collars so stiff they were afraid to swallow, would march down the aisle in church to the altar where the bishop would pronounce them adults in the eyes of the church. Ruthanne would be there as part of the Confirmation class. Their families would be there. Most of the town would be there. It was the closest thing Collie could get to a wedding.

Just before suppertime she peeked in the window at the office of Arthur J. Bent, General Contractor, and found everything in order. The secretary had gone home at four-thirty as she did every day, and Mr. Bent, as he did every day, picked up his newspaper, folded it to the sports page, and went to the john. The moment he was out of sight Collie pushed up the partly opened window. Leg over sill, she slid in. She hadn't much time. Darting like a cat, she removed Mr. Bent's desk key from its hiding place under the blotter and unlocked the bottom left drawer. As she'd hoped, the whiskey bottle was nearly empty. The cap came off easily. She reached into her pocket for the white hand-kerchief borrowed from her mother's bedroom bureau: inside the handkerchief was the white powder she had ground up from the nerve pills Clare kept in the medicine chest for the times Aunt Juney came to visit and had one of her bad headaches. They'd never been called anything but Aunt Juney's nerve pills. Two pills never failed to produce a strange change in Aunt Juney's behavior: her eyes would take on a glassy, blank look and her words would come out slurred and she wouldn't be able to walk without holding on to furniture. The effect usually lasted half a day. Be-cause Mr. Bent was a man and larger than Aunt Juney,

Collie had taken four pills, now ground to a thin white powder, which she poured into the bottle of whiskey. She saw with satisfaction that the powder blended in perfectly. She replaced the cap and wiped it clean before putting the bottle back in the drawer. She locked it and put back the key. At the sound of the flushing toilet, she hurried out the way she had come in, closing most of the window behind her.

There was only one thing Ruthanne Bent's mother had ever complained about, had ever hated, had ever become speechless with rage about, and that was liquor. Mrs. Bent allowed a glass of sherry after Sunday dinner, and not a drop else. Mrs. Bent was fond of telling people that, unlike other wives, she never had to worry about her husband doing that most odious thing—drinking liquor. What Mrs. Bent did not know, what Collie knew because she had been watching Mr. Bent for weeks, was what Mr. Bent did every day before he left his office.

She smiled a nervous smile as Mr. Bent poured himself a drink. It was dangerous to be spying through the window, but she couldn't bring herself to leave. The pills, once inside Aunt Juney, took about twenty minutes to act. She couldn't be sure if they would do the same with Mr. Bent. She wanted to be sure. There was one more step to the plan, but she knew she must be cautious.

In his office Mr. Bent quietly emptied the bottle, licking his lips as he put it down.

Just a few minutes later Collie stood at the telephone booth across the street, dialing the still-familiar number.

Her heart was thumping. Her stomach suddenly turned over and thudded to her knees. Moths seemed to have gathered in her chest. For the hundredth time that day she told herself that what she was doing was not a sin, was not truly wrong, but as the familiar voice at the other end of the line came on in greeting, she prayed a quick and silent purgatory prayer just to be certain. She covered the phone receiver with the handkerchief, cleared her throat, and prayed her voice would not fail her.

"Is this the Bent residence?"

"Yes, it is," said Ruthanne.

"You don't know me, but . . ."

"Hello? Speak up, I can't hear you. Who is this?"

Collie raised her whisper a tiny degree. "You don't know me, miss, but I assure you I'm a friend. Are you the wife of Arthur Bent?"

Ruthanne giggled. "No, I'm his daughter."

"May I speak to your mother, miss?"

"She's at the store right now. Who is this? I can tell her to call you back."

"Quite all right, quite all right, miss." Collie relaxed. She was almost enjoying herself. "Just a message from a concerned friend. I don't want to start any trouble, but I think you should know that Mr.—I mean your father—well, dear, your father is having a bit of a problem with something."

Ruthanne gasped. Collie gulped deeply and plunged in. "Take it from a friend! Arthur Bent will die of drink if he doesn't watch himself!"

Ruthanne gave a cry of surprise. Collie hung up quickly.

Her hands were shaking violently. Quickly she ran across the street again, ducking behind a tree as Mr. Bent came out of his building. He appeared to be having a difficult time standing in an upright position. He made it to his car, where he fumbled for a long time with his keys. It seemed he couldn't get the door open. Then the keys slipped out of his hands to the ground just under the car. Collie left him on his hands and knees, still fumbling. Then she ran back to the telephone booth to call the police. She didn't bother disguising her voice and she didn't leave her name. She reported very matter-of-factly that she was a concerned citizen who had just passed by a very drunk man, and gave the address. Breathlessly, she hurried home to get ready for Confirmation night.

Inside the church every mahogany arch, every marble apostle, every white pillar convoluting toward heaven, shimmered in the light of a hundred candles. Shadows rode puffs of summer-night air, drifting in and out of the confessional boxes and playing hide-and-seek in the folds of Our Lady of Perpetual Help's blue dress. There was a hush everywhere, a special, awesome hush, for the bishop came only once every three years. It was a silence that deepened and thickened as the people, their faces clean and shining, came tiptoeing into the church. Little children opened their mouths in amazement when they saw the altar, for the nuns had been decorating all day. It looked like a birthday cake. Mrs. Bent was the last one in. She was alone, and the whole town knew why. With a slight breezy energy the truth stole out in whispers up and down the pews: what a disgrace it was, Arthur Bent drunk like that in the middle of the day! And Confirmation Day, of all times! Everyone claimed to have seen him for themselves, staggering up the street to his house, belching as if it were the Fourth of July. Poor Mrs. Bent, everyone said.

Outside on the Confirmation line, gowns were adjusted and caps set on straight. Cameras clicked and flashbulbs popped. A girl shrieked when a boy snapped her garter belt. Ruthanne Bent left her place in line and scooted over to Collie. Her eyes were red and puffy. Keeping her head lowered, she said in a very low voice the thing Collie wanted most in the world to hear.

"I was wrong. I-I'm sorry." The line was straightening itself out with a flurry of anticipation. Ruthanne stood very still, her fingers clenched at the cuffs of her white gown. She reminded Collie vaguely of an angel in a Nativity scene.

Collie let her eyes open in surprise and confusion. "Ruthie, what's the matter? You look terrible." Seeing the tears about to splash, Collie quickly added, "You're not sick, are you?"

Ruthie shook her head slowly. "It's my father. I mean, I found out something today. What I was wrong about is believing my father when he said that your father is a—"

Collie touched Ruthanne's arm lightly, hushing her before Ruthanne could say the word. "You don't have to tell me anything, Ruthie." The line began to move down the sidewalk toward the church. Ruthanne took a deep breath.

"Maybe we can meet at the Pines tomorrow, Colleen?" At last Ruthanne looked up, her eyes squinting a hopefulness that made Collie flutter. She flashed Ruthanne a quick smile and nudged her back to her own place in line. It had worked.

The line proceeded with a strange, solemn importance. A thin breeze caught the skirt of Collie's gown and sent it rippling against her first pair of nylon stockings. On the top step outside the church she paused and looked up at the twilight sky, where a faint orange tint was floating on an unending stretch of pale blue. The organ processional was booming. The church's steeple reached upward like a finger, as if it meant to pluck some wonderful treat out of the air. It was difficult to believe that at any moment Russian bombers might appear, tearing the world asunder.

Chapter six

It was cold for October. Climbing up rickety ladders they borrowed from each other, the men took down the window screens. They held the glass panes high above their heads and shouted down for the children to hold the ladder straight or else. They poked their heads inside chimneys and pulled out sparrows' nests, tossing them to the wind even though the children cried. Standing on the roofs picking straw and dust from their sweatshirts, they were enormous, they were proud and brave, they were yelling for their wives to come have a look. Holding the ladders, the children shrieked that the sky was too blue. It hurt their eyes. When that was finished, the men swept the leaves to the front of their houses, and while they turned their backs, the leaping children scattered the piles. Braver ones, the ones whose fathers showed them how to inch along the edge of a roof like a man on a tightrope, dived in bottoms first. Oh, it don't hurt a bit they said, rubbing themselves, running off laughing when their fathers shouted, with fists raised, how they'd have to do it all over. But there was laughter in the shouts too, for the men were drinking beer. Every time a man looked ready to haul off a rake to a child's backside, the child ran to the icebox for another. They shook the bottles behind their backs so that when their fathers popped them open, foam oozed over their thumbs. Up and down the hill children pleaded to lap it up. It gets in your nose, they said. Oh, it tickles!

In her room facing the street Collie covered her ears, wishing she lived in a desert. The last of the leaves were clinging like drowners to maples ransacked by wind and grubby boys. They seemed forlorn. Sad and lonely. Empty branches rattled one against the other as mothers called their families home for lunch. It was a desolate time of year, she thought. It was squalid. Beside her, a whistling Mary sent her yo-yo on a loop-de-loop, round-the-world, all-the-way-to-China.

"Oh, get out of here," said Collie. "Why can't people leave me alone?"

Sighing, she licked the tip of her pencil and pressed it to the page.

Dear Ruthie (and she began again the letter bobbing about in her head through a summer spent lying on her back daydreaming in the Bent bomb shelter; through the early weeks of a new classroom; through night after night of fretful dreams her mother mysteriously attributed to a thing called the Curse) Dear, dear Ruthie, How are you? I am fine.

Muttering profusely, Collie crossed it out. You can't

very well say "how are you" to a person you saw an hour ago, or "I'm fine" when you wished yourself dead.

Dear Ruthie, Did I ever tell you how wonderful it is to be best friends with you? I have forgotten all about our fight and from the bottom of my heart forgive you for saying my father is a Communist. We have grown older and these things as they say fall by the way to either sprout or turn into prickles. Why won't you tell me how you found out your father is a liar?

Dear Ruthie, I understand why you can't tell even me how you found out your father is a liar. My mother says what goes on in a house stays in a house too. However

Dear Ruthie, Are you absolutely sure you love me better than anyone in the whole world? I certainly hope so because when I tell you what I have to tell you you're probably going to

Dear Ruthie,

Dearest Ruthie, best friend in the whole world, I won't blame you one bit if you hate me when I tell you

Dear sweet wonderful Ruthanne,

Cursing, Collie swept the mound of crumpled pages from her desk to the mound steadily growing on the floor. There was no use, she thought, in trying to say what she meant. Better to say what she wanted Ruthie to hear. Why bother with Truth, she wondered, chewing on her pencil, when all Truth did was make trouble? After all, it was the sentiment that counted most. One ought to be charitable.

Darling Ruthie, The day you turned your back on me was the saddest day of my life. For months I prayed you'd love me again and end my terrible strife. Imagine my joy when you came to me

No, growled Collie with irritation, this won't do. This won't do at all.

Dearest Ruthanne, Mercy as they say is never strained, for it drips down freely like the rain. Will I forgive you? Of course I will, and be your best friend forever, until

Collie groaned. Her teeth closed hard round her pencil. How was it that in books people got onto the page exactly what they wanted to say? Everywhere one looked were words of pain and sorrow and joy and Truth appearing as naturally as the leaves swaying one moment from the tips of branches and the next blown carelessly to the ground. Why there and not here?

Biting her pencil, she drew the blinds and fixed in her mind the idea of friendship being a leaf in the wind, rustling softly, billowing like a flag, extending outward, changing colors, blazing magnificently—and like it or not raked under some hoe and swept into a heap to be burned.

Damn! she said as her pencil shattered. Double damn! as she picked splinters of wood from her lips. Still, she wished there were a word for "heavy weight that sits in the belly like undigested food." If she knew one she'd write it down, find the words that explained it more, and run straight to Ruthanne with a poem.

Somehow she had to tell it. Clean it out the way she picked clean the twisting old roots of the cemetery pine trees when dead needles and the shreds of other people's litter gathered there. It was a kind of housekeeping, getting the muck out of the trees. Sometimes she got down on her knees with a little brush made of fresh pine branches, and swept the bottoms of the trunks. Bird droppings, the dried bodies of dead spiders, the hard globs of old sap, it was

45

incredible to think how much junk could wreck the look of a pine tree, and wasn't a sin just like that? Judas had got Jesus with a kiss. Into His hands went the nails. All for a lie, His Life for a lie, for after all, what Judas was doing was lying: an unspoken lie, a kiss.

But was it a lie, truly a lie, if Ruthanne didn't know in the first place?

She flung herself across her bed, hollering into her pillow.

Chapter seven

Except for a pewful of old women muttering into their rosary beads, the church was empty. Lit only by the red-cupped Vigils flickering their taste-of-purgatory flames, it rushed at Collie like sleep the moment she stepped in the door. Though she walked on tiptoe, the floors creaked. Though she kept her eyes straight ahead, glued to the shrine of perpetual devotion housing the sacred ciborium housing the Eucharist (Jesus have mercy, Jesus have mercy, sweet Son of Mary have mercy on me, said every footstep), fourteen stations of the cross leaped off their perches to clutch her by the throat. She hastened, head slumped, to the confessional box and slid back the thick velvet drapes. Kneeling, she pressed her face to the prayer screen and rapped politely, hoping the priest (Father Cavill was past sixty and liked his afternoon nap) had gone home. But no, there was the board sliding back with a thud, and there was the dim hulking figure inside, and here was her own small weak voice quivering like a leaf in the rain,

"Bless me, Father, for I have sinned." (This time I'll tell. I will, I will, I will.) The leather cushion beneath her knees felt wonderfully cool and comfortable. The hard oak of the confessional box enclosed her furiously thumping heart and hushed it.

"It has been one year and four months since my last confession." Cupping her hands, she imagined her soul borne up, up, up on magnificent silent wings to be hung like a rag at the feet of Our Lord and thoroughly shaken clean. She sighed profoundly.

"These are my sins."

Abruptly, so abruptly she nearly toppled backward, the massive shape on the other side of the grille came closer, emitting a long low chuckle that rattled her very bones.

"Colleen Dutton, are ye bein' off on a story again? Why, ye were in here only last Sadderdey!"

The priest laughed heartily. A hot blush spread over Collie's face. Her fists dug into her hipbones.

"D'ye think I'm one o' the sisters pattin' yer head fer yer tales? G'won now, girlie, start off the way it be, fer the Lord likes teh keep things in order."

With tremendous effort Collie gathered herself and forced her voice forward.

"N-no, Father, I mean it's not a lie, Father. Not really, Father, you see there's this sin I never confessed and . . ."

His hoarse guffaw seemed to explode from some frightening new depth of the confessional box. It was hot in there. It was stifling. Collie closed her eyes, feeling dizzy.

"G'won an' do it right, Colleen, or I'll be havin' ye do me a rosary."

The kneeler smelled like old sneakers. Its wood reeked of the sweat of a thousand grimy clutching fingers. Collie found it impossible to breathe.

"Well, g'won now, girlie, I haven't all day."

She clasped her hands together tightly. I won't weaken, she thought; oh God, don't let me weaken or faint, please please please please.

"Bless me, Father, for I have sinned. It has been one week since my last confession. These are my sins."

"There ye be now, girlie. What the Lord loves is the truth. What'd ye do this week, eh? Did ye go an' be touchin' yerself where ye oughtn't, eh?"

Collie felt her flush deepen, felt prickles race down her back, down the edge of her spine, down her legs to her knees, which might at any moment give way. She bit her tongue and covered her face with her fists.

"Father, I-I-I . . ."

"Out with it, girlie. The Lord knows it already now, don't He? An' how'll the good Lord be forgivin' ye when ye won't loose yer tongue an' say it, eh? Eh?"

I won't cry, she thought, squeezing her hands to her eyes. I won't cry, I won't, I won't, for then he'll come out of his seat and he'll put his fat hairy arms round me and I'll smell his mouth, his old stale mouth, no I won't cry, I won't, I won't."

"Ye well in there, girlie?"

"Y-yes, Father."

"Out with it, then. The Lord He loathes a lingerer, fer

the divil's the one wastin' time. Though ye be feelin' shame fer the tellin', twern't nothin' teh the fires o' hell. Out with it, girlie. Did ye be doin' that thing I said? Eh? Yis, did ye say? Sure an' if ye be wantin' the grace o' the Lord, Colleen, ye bist be tellin' me."

Through the grille flashed the white of his ear, came the sharp intake of his breath, and with a groan Collie buried her face in her arms as though it might keep him from hearing her weeping.

Mary Dutton was lying on her bed shooting crumpled balls of paper at the bucket suspended from the ceiling by means of kite string wound elaborately round its rim when Collie wandered in. What a hovel of a room, she said in disgust. What a disgrace to have for a sister a common barnyard beast content to roll about in her own muck— what a place, what a swine, what a muck! Promptly she was slammed in the face. Seeing it was only a wad of paper, she wailed she'd been hit in the eye and would be evermore blinded. Seeing it was paper covered in her own handwriting, covered with her innermost secret thoughts, she flung herself upon her sister and grabbed a handful of flesh.

Mary swung out heavily, scooped Collie by the legs and tumbled her to the floor. In a frenzy they rolled about, smacking skin, yanking hair, wrenching fingers, kicking, scratching, cussing. She was nimble but Mary was strong: for every blow Collie threw, she got three.

"There," said Mary, who with a final heave plopped down on her sister's stomach, "say Auntie three times and I'll let you go."

Collie squirmed. The grim hands locked round her wrists tightened their squeeze a turn between play and death. The legs pressed to hers clamped harder. Gloatingly, Mary tossed back her head and laughed. There was a ferocious glint in her eyes, a swell of pride in her cheeks.

"Sissypriss got rubber bones! Sissypriss got rubber bones! Siss——"

Calmly Collie spat in her eye. Thump! went the fist in her ribs. Doubling in pain, she shut her eyes, letting her body go limp. Her head rolled to the side.

"Don't fake me out, Collie," Mary breathed in her ear. "Just say Auntie one time and I'll quit. Okay? Okay? Coll? Hey, Coll? C'mon, Collie, I didn't mean hurting you. Anyway you started it, Coll. Hey open your eyes! Coll!"

The instant those fingers let go Collie sprang and toppled her sister over. With a yelp, Mary brought her down again and they tumbled in a heap to the doorway before the furiously tapping feet of their mother.

Arms across her chest Clare eyed them coldly. "And you dare call yourselves *girls?*" she said.

Chapter eight

 In the autumn dusk the men lit the fires. Up and down the hill flames danced, each higher than the one before it, filling the children's noses with crisp toasty smells and their hearts with fear the houses would catch it. Some ran, eyes dancing, for their water pistols or their mothers. Martin Dutton reached into a tree and brought down a long, curling, bare branch. He broke it up, scraped off the bark, and stuck marshmallows on the tips. Mary nearly burned off her hair, cooking over the fire. Gooey white stuff dribbled down her chin as she held out a stick to her sister.

"Don't want none," Collie grumbled, hugging her knees. "Just leave me alone, I said."

Over her head her parents exchanged looks. "Well after all she's near that time," whispered Clare. "Lord, how I wish she were grown and already married!"

Collie stared hard at the flames licking the black night sky. She wondered how it could be for a soul to feel the pain of the fires when being a spirit it had no flesh. Leaves burn, and in their place came ashes—ashes to ashes, dust to dust, said the priest, from dust thou camest to dust thou shalt return, do you think your bones will last forever? One gasps a last gasp and in that gasp one's soul slips out of the lips forever. Ah she died with her mouth open, said the old women lapping up their tea, she died with her mouth open, she's gone straight to the Lord, if you thought to look out the window, child, you would've seen her soul on its flight to heaven.

No, it couldn't be. They thought her a child and told her children's stories. A soul is invisible. It is shapeless and colorless. It is that part of a person which is God. It is God putting into you a piece of Himself, God who is everywhere except in hell, where His Light never reaches the darkness.

If hell is fire, how can it be dark? Because the sinner is blinded, that's why. The soul of the sinner is plunged for-evermore into darkness you can imagine yourself some night in your bed after the lights are out when there's no moon, no stars. If you press your fingers to your eyes you say, Ah this is what it is like then, imagining the house caught on fire and you tucked in so tight you can't bend a knee let alone escape and once the flames eat away your skin, your bones, what's left of you is your soul, that part of you which is God Himself.

But if God is my soul and there's no God in hell, how can it be that—Oh, I know why, thought Collie miser-ably, pressing her face to her knees; it's all because I'm a sinner, a sinner with a soul so besmirched that the light of my faith has been extinguished, oh God!

Thou who question the work of the Lord speak with the tongue of the devil. Thou who . . .

AHrrrr-AWK!

AHrrrr-AWK!

AHrrrr-AWK!

In her own ears it sounded, AHrrrr-AWK AHrrrr-AWK, and her heart took a leap and stood still. *Was it bombs or fire?* the children squealed as the men cocked their heads, counting signals. When they took out their wallets for the signal cards they all knew it was fire. But by the time the men ran to their houses for boots someone came by shouting never mind, nothing but a false alarm, and Collie found it in her to breathe once more.

Life is just like that for a sinner, thought Collie, as his cries echoed down the hill.

An arm came round her shoulder, and another one.

"When I was a girl the old women, your Nana's aunts, said you could look into the ashes of autumn leaves and tell your future," said her mother. Her mother was wearing her father's red wool coat. It dragged on the ground like a blanket. She unbuttoned the front and pulled Collie inside and buttoned it up again. Her mother's heart ticked into her spine and she nestled herself against her. This is what a kangaroo feels like, thought Collie. Why can't I be a kangaroo?

She shivered. "What did they say your future would be, Mummy?" It was years since she'd called her Mummy unless she was sick, and was embarrassed. Though she'd said it, she could no more imagine her mother a girl than she could those leaves in one piece back on the trees where they belonged or her own soul shining clean. She was glad her face wasn't showing.

"Well, they looked into the ashes and they poked around with sticks, and they said to Mumma—'course they wouldn't be talking to me since all I knew was English— they said to Mumma, God rest her soul, there's a fine girl you've got there, Elena. One day she'll be Mumma to a girl the likes of which the world's never seen."

"Oh, Mummy, they didn't say that," said Collie, squirming impatiently. "You're making that up 'cause you want me to laugh."

"Oh yes they did, Colleen Elena Dutton. I can see them same as if it was yesterday, bowing their backs down low, reading the future in those leaves. Your Nana stood there with her hands on her hips, nodding away like a pigeon when they said I'd have a daughter fit for a prince. Why, when I was carrying you your Nana'd press her ear to my belly and say how right they were, for sure as she had ears she could hear a princess kicking!"

Pushing backward, Collie popped open all the buttons of the red coat. "Oh Mummy, I'm not good! They were wrong! I'm not good at all!"

With a wise smile Clare held her tightly. The last of the leaves turned themselves inside out and disappeared. Through hot watery eyes Collie watched until only a faint red glow was left. Then came her father's footsteps, and she was swung through the air in his arms as easily as if she were cloth.

"Oh Daddy, put me down! I'm too big to carry!" She pinched herself, for it was years since she'd called him

Daddy. She was glad her face was hidden away in the bulge of his shoulder.

"Your Nana was the happiest lady in the world, the day you were born," said Clare upstairs, pulling the blanket up under her chin. She pushed back a knot of damp twisted hair and kissed her mouth warmly. "You were always her favorite, you know, Colleen. Don't you recall your Nana at all?"

Slurping up their tea from the saucers, the old wrinkled cats of the aunts said in English, they must have said it in English or else how would she have known, "Praise God she died with her mouth open."

Crossing her fingers so it wouldn't be a lie, she turned to the wall. How could she remember somebody who died when she was too little? Why bring it up, for God's sake, when it didn't make any sense? Her mother, bending down, touched her hair and her neck as though feeling for fever. Collie cringed. Why couldn't people leave her be when all she wanted was to sleep? Clare sighed and left her alone in the darkness.

Her mouth was open and there it was. Open as if she were trying to talk but the words couldn't get out; open as if she were surprised to find herself there; a round open O of a mouth, a wondering red circle, and staring at it, Collie had seen where the gold tooth was—her only jewel but for her Colleen—and had seen the trickle, now foamy white, now bright hot red, running down the sides where the lips had parted. What she had heard was the terrible silence when no words came, though she tried and she tried and she tried.

Collie filled her ears with her fingers and passionately wished herself asleep. She turned on her side. She bent up her knees. She flattened herself again, imagining herself weightless on a huge fluffy cloud, floating above the green trees that were straining to touch her.

How could you do this to me, the mouth was saying. All this time I thought you were a good girl.

She concentrated on her shoulders, relaxing them, melting them into the bed, into the soft white depths of the cloud.

Oh! How could you do this to me?

Blue the sky was, miles and miles of empty blue. Below her, men perched on roofs, the summer screens in their hands. Hello! Hello! she called, waving. One by one the rooftops parted: opening, opening, opening.

How could you do this to me?

Please God make me go to sleep. Oh my God each breath I take I take for Thee. Look down upon Your servant Lord and make her full of Thee. I know I am but weak and wrong, not better than a flea, but with Your Love O Lord I'm strong and in You let me be.

The wind howled and the windows shook. She snuggled under her blankets. Come, sleep, come. She sniffed sleep and hurried after it. But sleep, hovering around her bed like a ghost, whistled in the windows and creaked on the floors. It scraped against the sides of the house and tapped on the rooftops like branches. She wrapped her arms around her head, as if that might help force her wild thoughts in one direction. She thought if only she could pin down one thought, if she could turn and twist it about in her mind, she could straddle that thought and ride it to sleep. All she had to do was gather herself. She thought how her father had raked the leaves. She would rake her thoughts like that. She flipped herself over and thought how splendid the trees had appeared, all colors, looking like they'd caught on fire. Yes that was it, that was good, trees looking like they'd just caught on fire, with their oranges and golds and yellows and reds—

> *Orange and golden and yellow and red,*
> *The trees catch fire this time every year,*
> *and send through the skies hot furious flames*

And send through the skies hot furious flames. It wasn't working. And send through the skies hot furious flames— it wasn't working at all, for she had died with her mouth hanging open. She had slumped to the floor and she lay there. Orange and golden and yellow and red the trees catch. She'd been alone in the yard. The trees were bare. The trees were black. Nana came to the window to wave. Look Nana, look, see what I'm making for you! It was winter. Those boys were hiding in the bushes. Orange and golden and yellow and black. Don't you say those terrible things! If you say those terrible things I'll hit you with my shovel! Yellow and red and white and black. If my Nana could hear you say those things she'd take Papa's strap to you! Orange and golden and yellow and running. Oh Nana! Where are you oh we can't play now, oh I didn't mean to do it don't be mad I told them to stop where are you oh Nana come orangeandgoldenandyellowandredorangeandgoldenandyellowandredorangeandgoldenand-spinning spinning spinning—

Faster and faster it spun, the thing she was on. She was clinging. Her hair blew back, whipping her face. Let go, let go! someone shouted, but she wouldn't let go no she couldn't let go she was holding something hard, it was holding her, a branch of a tree, a tree she had climbed, hello! hello! she called. People below craned their necks, pointing, how brave she is, how strong, how the wind whips about her yet still she holds on, holds it like a pole on a tightrope, the handle of her shiny red shovel. Stop that. Stop that right now or I'll hit you I will! There was a face an ugly face saying awful things, things you could go to hell for saying. There's my Nana in the window—if she could hear you —that's my Nana you're talking about don't you say those things I'll hit you with my shovel I will spinning and spinning and spinning around faster and faster and faster she was tumbling she was head over heels through the air oh I'm falling I'm falling

Thud. All was smashed to a dark hard silence. This is a dream. This must be a dream. If this weren't a dream I would see, I would hear. Feet. Feet running. This isn't a dream. Voices. Who? Here I am! Over here! Voices calling through miles and miles, Collie, here Collie, here! This must be a dream or you'd see me. Collie! Come, Collie, come! This must be a dream or I'd feel, I'd feel where my arms and my legs are, oh where are they I must have lost them when I fell. Oh that hurts, don't pull me like that. This isn't a dream. Oh don't.

Collie! Collie, wake up! Hurry, Coll, get up!

Stop that!

Collie, you'll miss it. Wake up!

She groped for the hard dark silence. It was better not to feel. It was the charitable thing.

Coll!

Wind rushed past. She was yanked upright. Oh why can't you leave me alone?

Hurry, Collie, you'll sleep right through it. Collie, the fire, hurry, Jake's place is on fire!

Fire. The flames, the hot furious flames. Orange and golden and yellow and red. Oh don't be mad, I didn't mean it!

Her eyes sprang open. Mary's face was white. Mary's eyes were sparking ferociously. She blinked, trying to focus. Gold flames danced in Mary's eyes. How did they get there?

I didn't. I didn't mean it, really I didn't. I told them—

Hurry, I said, or you'll miss it!

She forced herself awake, shoving her arms through the sleeves of the coat. Red. Orange and golden. She was pulled to her feet. She was dragged downstairs, then outside, where the hot furious flames were everywhere. She covered her face with her hands and fell in a heap to the ground.

Chapter nine

At the stove Clare stirred milk with a long wood spoon. It was no wonder nobody could sleep, what with all the excitement. Poor Jake, him just putting in a new countertop. Why, that restaurant was an institution gone thirty years! Surely it'd go up again. Jake was a Trombley; those Trombleys never took misfortune lying down. My, though, wasn't it frightening to think any minute it could've spread? Why, it could've been our house if the wind had shifted!

Collie watched the hand on the spoon circling the pot. She rested her elbows wearily on the table. Her mother sounded far away, a bird flying high above the house, cawing faintly, now and then swooping lower, as though it desperately meant to find something.

"Martin, feel that girl's head. I swear she's got a fever coming on."

"I'm fine."

Her father had not washed his face. He was blackened,

grimy. No one had known where Jake was when the fire
started. Holding their hands to their faces, the men had
plunged into the smoke, once, twice, three times. It cackled
awfully. It hissed. A wall crumbled like tissue paper.
Though they didn't say so, they thought Jake was burned
alive. No, there he was, there was Jake, pulling on his coat
behind him. All the time the roof was caving in, the walls
were folding, the glass of the windows was flying everywhere, Jake in his bewildered way was flinging his arms
about, telling anyone who'd listen how he'd been just down
the road for a quick game of gin. The neighbors patted his
back; they said they'd have a raffle, a big do, get the place
back proper, it was a miracle the other houses weren't
touched, though it'll be a hellofa job cleanin'. Good thing
gravestones are made o' stone; the cemetery only got
most o' the cinders. They had looked at Jake with new eyes
for he could have been burned alive. Nobody knew how it
started. The fire trucks never looked as big in the station,
as they did on your own street practically in front of
your own house. Anything could've started it. Anything.
Somebody's leaves still smolderin' or greasy rags in the
cellar. Butts not put out proper. "Don't worry, old boy,
we'll have a do. Whole town'll turn out," they said. The
smoke curled into the sky, the pealing sky. It was thunder,
it was fireworks, it was burning, it was magnificent, it was
because Collie had wished it, that's what. She was the one
who hated Jake. He'd turned her out. She'd got Arthur
Bent and she'd got Jake Trombley. He could have been
burned alive. No, she hadn't meant for that. Ruthie said
Mr. Bent threw up till he turned blue. Well, my Daddy'll

never as long as he lives touch another drop. Good thing too. He could've died. One drop more and he could have died, she said. It was a funny thing how somebody could live or die on account of you. Dear Ruthie, I could have killed your father. But I didn't. Aren't you glad? I killed before and I could do it again. It's easy. I'm not good like you think I am. If you could x-ray my soul you'd see. Don't tell anyone, they'll put it in the newspaper and my mother will cry and say how she can't hold up her head.

"She's tired, that's all, tired and worn," said her father, touching her face. His fingers pressed against her cheek, lightly, coolly. It was astonishing to her how those were the same fingers that had snapped the branch of a tree, that an hour ago had mastered the heavy fire hose, battling the flame and the smoke, and now touched her so impossibly gently. How would that hand respond if it knew it was touching something bad, something rotten to its very core?

"Give her some milk, Clarey. She'll feel better."

I will protect my parents, Collie thought. They are good. And my little sister Mary, who is much better than me. Mary is good. It's hard to be good. They'll never know. She cupped her head with her hands. It was very heavy; it was hard to hold it still. Easier to let herself fall, to sleep.

Before her was a steaming cup. Drink, her mother was saying, her voice dim and muffled. Drink before it's cold. Mustn't let it get cold. Two things there are: hot and cold. The fire was hot. You could feel your face smart even standing on the steps of your own house. Red and hot. The milk was white. White and hot. Not cold, not cold like a hand dangling limply that was the same as touching ice. Collie closed her fingers round the cup, but as she raised it to her lips she saw that inside was foamy stuff trickling down the corners of the parted lips that would not, would not speak. Any moment it would turn red, hot red. With a cry, she thrust the cup away and buried her face in her arms.

"I told you she's sick," said Clare. "Let's get her back to bed. If she's not running a fever now, she'll have one in the morning."

Her feet were cold. The sheets were hot. Then her feet were hot and the sheets were cold. She closed her eyes. Her eyes were hot. There were those two things: cold and hot.

Her mother brought flowers, fat white flowers she called snowdrops, and Collie forced herself to smile. She could not look at them for long. They looked cold.

A nurse brought soup, clear broth in a plastic cup that might melt. Collie sniffed it and pushed it away. Oh but you have to eat sweetie said the nurse, who had a large red face and smelled like everything else in the hospital. The nurse had no fingernails. Her fingers seemed to have been chopped off at the tips. Collie, thinking that was strange, wanted to ask why but her mouth was full of the broth. It was hot. She spat it out. It was too hot. The nurse's face got redder. She looked ready to burst. She looked hot.

Her father brought a box of soft ice cream. Sitting on the

edge of the bed, he was reading from a book. Holding the book in his enormous hands, he read:

> Should you ask where Nawadaha
> Found these songs so wild and wayward,
> Found these legends and traditions,
> I should answer, I should tell you,
> "In the bird's nests of the forest . . ."

As he read the lines she'd loved as a very small child, he held to her mouth the sweet white ice cream, the stuff she loved any other time not this time. It was cold. It was too, too cold. Her father let it melt the way she liked it so she could hold it to her lips and drink it, but it was cold, too too cold. She peered at her father, who was holding his book, and tried to understand what he meant when he said

> Love the sunshine of the meadow,
> Love the shadow of the forest

but they meant nothing, nothing at all. They were words without meaning, they were hot words. Too too hot.

Mary was crying. Why should Mary cry? Mary was good. Don't cry, Mary, she wanted to say. Mary climbed onto the bed and lay beside her. Tears spilled onto her face. They were hot. Mary lifted her hand and enclosed it. Mary's fingers were cold. Too cold. The hot tears touched her face while the cold fingers touched her hand. Mary was hot and cold at the same time. How could that be?

In the night, shadows clumped in the corners. The shadows looked like a beast. The shadows scampered and rushed at the bed. Collie screamed. Something came and drove the beast away. In the corner huddled an old woman, rubbing her hands together to keep warm. Are you cold, Collie wanted to say. I know all about cold. The old woman in the corner wrapped a shawl around herself. It fell off. Hot to cold. All the night the old bent woman pulled her shawl around her and all night it slipped back off. Collie watched with interest.

Her mother's eyes were sunken and dark. Surely if they sank any more they would disappear. There were the eyes sinking and here were her mother's hands all around her, doing things that felt nice. Warm. Her mother's hands were warm. But there were the eyes dark and deep; her mother's eyes were not hot, not cold, they were sinking and dark and deep. Put them back, Mummy, she tried to say, but when she heard her own voice she was surprised when all it made was a long low groan. It was full of awfulness, her own voice. She thought how bad she must be to make a noise like that, and was ashamed.

One day it was sunny. The sun came in the window and rested on her face. It was warm. She drew herself to a little ball and curled up in the warmth. Sun, she thought, trying to touch it. Sun. She felt the word on her tongue. She rolled it around and pressed it against her teeth. It felt good. "Good," she murmured, feeling her voice warm in her throat and her mouth, "good."

One week later she was well enough to write again.

Dear Ruthie, Thank you one thousand and one times for

making me all those pictures. The ones I was too sick to look at when you brought them are all around me now. My mother pinned some on the walls and I keep the rest under my pillow. My favorite one is the one of Sister Mary Theodora with a pumpkin head. How do you get the eyes to look like that? I wish I wasn't so clumsy so I could draw too. Do you like me the way I am? Are you sure? Let's be best friends forever, even when we get married. I think we should marry brothers so we can be sisters-in-law, and have houses next door to each other. I'm not going to have children but I'll help you take care of yours. Okay? I'm feeling lots better but my mother won't let me out of bed yet. You know how my mother is. Write to me during Geography, you can hold the book up straight and gorilla-face Theodora won't know. Write to me in Penmanship too, and Recess. You can give the letters to Mary, okay? Love, Colleen.

P.S. Are you one hundred percent sure you like me better than anyone, because Mary said she saw you with Isabella Potter yesterday and you were also sitting next to her at lunch where I usually sit. I said it's only because I'm not there. Is it?

P.P.S.S. Do you think I'm a good person? If you do, why?

Then she lay on her back listening to rain on the roof, straining every bit of herself in the listening, looking for a word to describe each drop and patter. It sounded like a child's fat fingers on a tin drum. It sounded like coffee perking in her mother's tall pot. It sounded like pebbles washed by waves onto other pebbles along a misty, gray, murmuring beach. It sounded like squirrels' feet on a hollow tree in the thick of a green dripping forest. It sounded most of all like rain falling relentlessly on the roof. Frowning, she seized her pencil.

Oh rain!
Washing everything clean
Oh rain!
What in the world do you mean?

She thought if she could concentrate hard and long enough she would understand its meaning. Everything had to have a meaning. It meant the clouds had filled with moisture and now were overflowing. It meant the ground would have its drink, the earth refresh itself to go on living. It meant the roof needed new shingles, for the rhythms were most peculiar and, as the rain fell, you could tell where birds had pecked, where last year's snows had stayed too long. It meant many things. The old man is snoring. Mary the Queen of Heaven has witnessed another entry to hell, and weeps. Out of Her tears grow the flowers, the tomatoes and peppers and figs. Is that fair? Or perhaps the rain meant nothing, another thing to wonder about when all there was to do was put up an umbrella or stay indoors. All the same, you couldn't help turning it over in your mind and solving it like a multiplication problem. If only Life were like that! On the other hand, there were things you couldn't possibly know till you're dead, so why bother? One thing was sure enough: there were the sounds of the rain, and the smells of the rain and the taste when you put out your tongue. Rain was one thing with a name and a look and a feel. Not like Life at all, or God. Good for rain, thought Collie, listening hard, for she desperately wanted to say in words exactly how those sounds were hitting the roof like a drum, like coffee, like pebbles, like squirrels on a hollow tree.

Drip, drop, went the rain. Pitter, patter. Splat. Drip drop pitter patter, splat. Drip drop pitter patter, splat. Drip drop pitter patter splish, splat. Steady as breathing. Well almost. It certainly was free to fall where it wanted. Unlike most other things. People, for instance. No matter what you want to do, there's sure to be someone trying to stop you. Nobody can stop rain. Not even with bombs. God could. Could God send rains so fierce He couldn't stop them? Oh why do I bring God into everything, why not leave God out of it for once? Better not say that. God is in all things. God is in rain. Every little drip and drop, and pitter and patter and splat. Of course. God is right here. Now. God hears all things, even thoughts. God, if You hear me, land a drop right here in the middle of the pane where not one drop has hit yet. I'll count to ten, then You land it, okay? One—two—oh better not do that. Surely it's a sign of doubt to do that. Thomas had to stick his hand in Jesus to make sure it was Him. The Doubter, he was. Everyone else said, Well now Jesus so You're back! Well I would have done that too. Would I? Oh I wish I was good! Rain is good. It has a look and a feel and a taste and a meaning. Jesus was good. Everyone says so, it must *be* so. But what is the point in thinking about God at all when you haven't even got an idea about what you're thinking about? What if somebody just made the whole thing up in the first place, like a story or a poem, and it sounded good, so people believed it. Or only good, the truly good people believed it. If you believed it, you knew for once and for all you were good.

 1963

Chapter ten

Things froze before Thanksgiving. Frost shimmied up the maple trunks, crept through black branches and erupted like exclamation points from the tips of startled twigs. No two icicles looked the same. Snow fell over the charred remains of Jake's Grille and covered the ground, as if nothing had ever been there. The lot was up for sale but nobody wanted it, for the place was jinxed. (Jake opened a Spa next door to the church and said how a man had a better perspective on things, being off the dizzying hill.) Either people died less in the winter, or cars didn't dare the heights, because funerals were scarce. Ruthanne said the caretaker's shed turned into a tomb until spring and if they went there they'd see corpses piled up with the shovels and lawnmowers. She didn't want to go. Let Colleen find some other girl who liked disgusting things; she was only saying what she heard. Anyway they couldn't get in if they'd wanted to; the fence was too high and they'd probably rip their clothes trying. The fence had gone up after the fire, a solid steel fence with spikes at the top and gates that mysteriously swung open on Sundays. The people thought it was a good thing, a thing they'd clamored years for, what with all the vandals sneaking up the hill from the project and tipping over graves in their drunken escapades and Lord knew what else went on. It was a terrible thing when you started letting outsiders, especially foreigners, into town. Nothing but nothing was sacred. Desecration went on all around, they said; though when Collie asked what that meant, they said it was the work of the devil and the Puerto Ricans. She'd never noticed a tipped grave. They said it happened in the night and was fixed by morning. All the same, it happened. In the spring they said the pines would come down, the graceful pines gathering in their boughs mounds of snow like women on their way to hang bed sheets to dry in the sun. Puerto Rican boys put beer bottles in the branches, they said, and did other things as well, and one day someone would catch them. Collie wrote a letter to the newspaper.

She wrote that it was a criminal thing, a thoughtless thing, a desecration, to chop down something as living as the pines in the cemetery circle. Those trees were older than anyone in town. They were a monument to beauty and to God. A thing of endless joy. Ever green and ever faithful they were; they strained toward God in the skies, never changing no matter the season. How sad to have them gone! Didn't the people know that every pine was nurtured by the tears of Our Most Holy Virgin weeping for our sins? Let him who was without sin swing the first ax!

The letter was sent off unsigned, and when it appeared,

bold and clear in print, Collie locked herself in her room to study every word. It gave her a queer sensation to know people picking up their newspapers would turn to this page (she imagined women putting down the afternoon laundry to remark what a fine letter it was, how they'd never thought of it quite that way but would now), and be touched by what she had written. Surely they would be touched, she thought. If the part about the monument didn't get them, then swinging the first ax would. She imagined Arthur Bent at the supper table, laying down his paper and rubbing his chin, saying, You know, dear, I ought to have some say in this business. After all, most of that concrete up there came from me. Yes, better that we leave the pines up. Read for yourself, dear, and see what I mean. You too, Ruthanne. It's a noble and sensible letter.

The pines would be saved and she would be a hero. An unsung one, which is humbler and better in the eyes of the Lord. No matter how loudly people called for the writer of the letter to come forward, she would hold her tongue. She looked in the mirror, cocking her head back and forth, staring into her own eyes and imagining people all over town applauding her letter, and wondering where it had come from, for never had they thought that any one of them could write so, so—Collie pursed her lips speculatively—so damn well good now, did they?

She skipped down to the supper table and got out the plates without being told. Her father came home and spread the paper on his knee. The letter was on page four and he took an unusually long time to get there. He clucked over last night's town meeting failing to get a quorum. He said how shocking it was that a fellow he knew from the K. of C. was arrested for drunken behavior; can't a fool keep his liquor indoors? He remarked on the price of beef and new uniforms for the high school band. He turned over a page and said wasn't that Clare's friend Ida behind the quilt booth at the church bazaar? Not a bad picture. Look, they raised a thousand dollars for Jake. Now he can pay off the new place. What's the matter, Colleen, got ants in your pants? That boy of Sam Connery's graduated, Clarey. First honors he took too. You remember him; he used to deliver the paper. Nice kid. Not a bit like his old man. Sit still, will you, Colleen, you're rattling the table. Now what's this? A criminal thing? A desecration? Collie forced her face into blankness and looked up in casual interest as her father read the letter aloud.

"Let him who is without sin swing the first ax, yours very truly, Anonymous. Not a bad effort, Colleen, not a bad effort at all," he said. His eyes were merry and proud.

Collie shrieked. There was no privacy in the world. She might as well live in a glass cage. They knew! Everyone knew. She was ruined.

Clare dumped the beans into a pot of boiling water and wiped her hands on the dishcloth, which was never far from her reach. "I like the part about the monument," she said, "but I wish you'd done it with rhymes, Colleen. If you ask me, a poem is ever so much more effective. People remember poems better, especially when they're short ones. Why didn't you put your name to it? Martin, don't you think she should've put her name to it?"

Martin nodded gravely.

"If it was a poem you could've got five dollars for it, Colleen. Buy yourself something pretty," added Clare.

"Bet they cut 'em down anyhow," said Mary bluntly, peering over her father's shoulder. "Kids at school told me not to tell you that. We read your letter at third recess. Anyway, everyone, even Sister, liked it."

Collie thumped her fist on the table and flew in a rage to her room. As long as she lived, she vowed into her pillow, she would not, would not, would not write one more word. It was too awful. It was humiliating. It was a desecration.

The river froze early. The sluggish gray river that curled between twin plastics factories, muddy and stinking and useless any other time of year, dressed itself like a stage. The ice glinted in the sun. Someone scraped away a snowbank and set fire to a mound of twigs. Skaters clomped to it, their faces crisp and pink, and peeled off their mittens to warm their icy hands. The air was full of electricity. It was pealing and tingling and achingly bright.

"C'mon," called Mary, wrapping her father's muffler round her neck. "Hurry, Coll, I'll race ya!"

Collie looked up, taller and braver in her skates. The thrill of anticipation lunged in her chest as she wobbled like a colt to the ice.

"Wait for me," pleaded Ruthanne, just arriving. She had waited to be driven by her father. Collie looked at her in dismay. Ruthanne was all blues and whites. Her head was covered in fluffy white fur, as though a kitten had attached itself to her hair. She wore a tight short dress of deep furry blue that pleated out around her skinny thighs. Her legs were coated with a leotard that perfectly matched the dress. White pompoms flounced on her skate laces. Her hands were thrust into a muff that matched her hat. Collie moaned.

"What's the matter, don't you think it's pretty?" Freckles leaping off her face in the sharp glare of the sun, Ruthanne veiled her eyes. The muff trembled.

" 'Course it's pretty, Ruthie. Real pretty. But what'd you go dressing like that for? We're here to skate, not march in a parade. Aren't you cold?"

Hurt, Ruthanne puckered her lips. She tossed back her head in a gesture unknown to Collie and squeezed her lips together. Collie held out a thick mittened hand and rubbed the muff awkwardly.

"It doesn't matter anyway, Ruthie," she lied. Mary skidded off the ice and bumped toward them, eyes bugging.

"Where you going, a circus? How you gonna skate in that?"

Ruthanne's lower lip protruded. A teardrop trickled. "There's nothing wrong about looking nice, is there?"

Mary snickered. Collie looked from one to the other and said her ankles hurt.

"She skates like a boy," said Ruthanne, watching Mary shove off, waving her arms for speed. Mary bent forward and sailed across the ice with a quick ease that made Collie jittery with delight. "Just look at her. Why can't she act like a girl?"

Demurely, Ruthanne tiptoed to the ice. She inched a skate forward as though stepping on glass.

"What's the matter with you, Ruthie? You didn't act like this last year. Are you gonna skate or not?"

"I suppose you want to do what your sister's doing." She waited for an answer. "Well, do you?"

Confused, Collie looked away at Mary playing kick-the-can far down the river. Mary's blades cut through the air and glided stunningly over the ice. She was having a wonderful time. What was wrong with that?

"All I can say, Colleen, is if you want to be childish like that, then you're *not* my friend!"

Mary was calling. Flying over the river, using her body like a boat, Mary was calling, C'mon, Coll, c'mon! Ruthanne moved forward as though her ankles were tied together. She wiggled, letting her short skirt flutter. Elbows bent, she held the muff close to her stomach, like a hot-water bottle. Twirling, she cut a tiny circle in the ice just off the shore and beamed at Collie proudly.

Certainly this was not Ruthanne, not the real Ruthie. There were her crooked eyes, her freckles, her funny bony jaw. Underneath the costume was Ruthanne. Her legs must be freezing.

"You ought to be ashamed of your sister, Colleen. Running around like a boy. Honestly, how can you be *seen* with her?"

Who put that tone, those words, in her mouth?

Standing on the river bank, Collie awkwardly kicked at the crusty snow, staring at Ruthanne as though she had never seen her before. Overnight, she had changed, changed as simply and surely as a maple tree in September. It wasn't possible, but there it was.

"We're much too old for that sort of thing, Colleen."

Ruthanne pressed her muff to her face, blinking her eyes in a rapid, odd way Collie had never noticed before. She found her voice.

"Cut it out, Ruthie. I want to skate."

A hand shot out of the muff, gripping her firmly by the arm. "I mean it, Colleen. If you go out there with those—those *children*—I'll never speak to you again!"

Collie gritted her teeth and looked away.

"Well?" The corners of Ruthanne's lips curled upward into two tight, tiny, hard knots. "To tell you the truth, Colleen, it really is embarrassing for me to be with somebody who's such a child. I can't believe it of you, I really can't."

"Lay off. I'm not a child."

Ruthanne laughed a cackly sort of low-pitched laugh through her closed lips. She tossed her head back, looking about at the same time to see if anyone else was watching her. "That's okay, Colleen. My mother said that some girls *mature* faster than others. You can't help it if you're slow."

On the ice the skaters were rushing past each other, yelping and laughing, and over their tomato-red faces their breaths flew like word-bubbles in the comics. Deep inside herself Collie felt a sudden wildness rising. Her body was aching to move, to shove itself off against the hard snow and soar. She could almost taste the wind in her mouth. She rose. Ruthanne backed away, as if she feared the change in Collie's expression. "Well, I didn't really mean you're *slow*, Colleen. Look, I'll let you wear my muff for a little while. Maybe your mother will get you one, too!"

"Get out of my way, Ruthie."

"Colleen! What do you mean? Hey! Where are you going? Colleen Dutton, if you go out there and skate like a boy, I'm leaving! I'm going home! Colleen—"

Ruthanne's voice dissolved, drowned by the rush of air as Collie went speeding down the ice, arms crooked at her sides the way Olympic skaters did it. Breaking clear of the other skaters, she shut her eyes, pumping her legs in a fury. When she looked again back toward the shore she caught a glimpse of Ruthanne wobbling away toward the road. The little skirt flounced up and down like a handkerchief.

At home her mother was ironing. Steam sizzled. The board creaked beneath her hands. Her father's shirts hung like clouds around the kitchen. Her mother was singing.

> *"Kay sirrah, sirrah!*
> *Whatever will be, will be,*
> *Will I be handsome?*
> *Will I be rich?*
> *Here's what she said to me:*
> *Kay sirrah, sirrah!"*

Collie dumped her skates on the floor. Her own smell of damp wool filled her with repulsion. She looked at her hands. They were chapped, raw, ugly. She slapped her legs. They were thick. She glanced down at herself: she was dumpy, awkward, a cow. She imagined her own face and saw it for what it truly was: ordinary, plain, too small, too round.

Her mother poured water into the iron. It spurted vehemently. "Did you have a good time?" she said.

Collie flared, fanning out in sudden fury. She stamped her foot. How could her mother, her very own mother, be so stupid? What a stupid thing to say! There she stood, ironing, without a care in the world. What did she know anyway? What a fool! And whirling, Collie lashed out at the shirts, sending an armful in a heap to the floor.

Clare set down the iron. "Young lady—young lady don't you go stomping into my kitchen—"

There it was again, that word: lady. It sounded like sipping from a tiny delicate teacup. It sounded like the flutter of moths' wings inside a jar. It sounded like the swish of Ruthanne Bent's skating skirt, lady, lady, lady—

Collie spun, ready to strike. Her mother caught her arm in midair and held it. For a long moment they stared at each other, one grim, the other panting.

"Don't-you-ever-call-me-that," hissed Collie through clenched teeth. Breaking free, she bounded away to her room, slamming the door behind her.

"Oh I do wish she was grown and married," said Clare when her husband came home. "You've no idea how unbearable it is."

After that she took great care to avoid Ruthanne's eyes. She stayed at their edges and tiptoed around their bright lapping pools. The way a little girl teases waves on a beach, she went forward, only to retreat the moment they touched her. They wanted to lap her up, those eyes. They wanted to pull her in. They were familiar eyes, not Ruthanne-familiar, but the eyes of women who sat in their kitchen asking, Did you have a good time? Are you good? They were greedy eyes that clutched at your words and strangled whatever you said. Now and then they would brighten. They would pick over what you said like fishing for sand dollars in a mound of dried seaweed and, grabbing what they wanted, they would call it their own. Most of what you said they tossed over their shoulders. There was little to please them. There was little they liked. To stir up the emptiness you must dance, you must sing, you must be pretty and funny and bounce off the chairs with cheer. It was not sadness in the eyes. It was not grief. It was worse. It was the look she had seen on dogs tied to a pole while their puppies scampered happily all around just out of their reach. Nana had it. Nana had been watching from the window while she was playing in the snow. Are you having a good time? Are you a good girl?

Are you, are you, are you? There were some boys hiding in the bushes. Nana in the window couldn't see them. Nana clutching her woolly house shawl round her thin shoulders stood in the window and couldn't hear what they said. Nana who loved her, who blew out bubbles of love for nobody but her own Colleen: there was Nana standing in the window of her big yellow house, all alone, the silence rubbing up against the glass panes like light, smoky fog. Out of the bushes came a growl, and Collie went stiff with fear. Up went her shovel like a sword—

Laying down the iron, her mother had it. Tell me, tell me, tell me. Slipping wire hangers in the sleeves of her husband's shirts, her mother seemed to ache with longing for some secret invisible thing dangling just out of her reach. As if Collie were the one who knew how to get it, her mother demanded and demanded and demanded to be told.

Where did you go? What did you do? Did you have a good time?

Nana never went anywhere beyond three or four streets bordering her own house, the house she had come to as a bride. She walked to the church, where she prayed in Italian over her rosary beads. She walked to the meat market, where she ordered, in musical English, sausage and gleaming, red slabs of meat. She walked to the little grocery store, where clerks she knew by name measured flour into cloth sacks and directed pungent wedges of yellow cheese through a grinder so shiny you could see your face in it. As if her blood depended on it, Nana would put the cheese gratings to her nose and sniff. She always found it acceptable, always said it was just the right thing. Often Collie suspected her grandmother had never learned the English to contradict. It was no use trying to get Nana to walk the extra block to the candy store or up the hill to Jake's for a soda. Nana's legs hurt all the time. Hidden behind ankle-long dresses in the winter and thick brown knitted stockings in the summer, Nana's legs had to be fussed over, worried about, propped up on a footstool before the rocking chair where Nana sat after shopping, asking in her peering way, Did you have a good time, *caramia?* Nana never talked about the old country and Collie never asked. When it was time for Grandpapa to come home from work, it was time for Collie to leave.

At home Grandpapa talked Italian. He smelled of men: leather and shaving lotion that came in through the back door every day at twenty minutes past six. On Christmases and Easters Grandpapa came for visits with five-dollar bills, and on Sundays Grandpapa stopped by the Dutton house with Hershey Kisses for the girls. In his stiff white shirt he stooped to allow Collie and Mary to kiss him. Otherwise, they stayed out of his way. In the company of anyone else, Grandpapa never addressed Nana. In the company of Grandpapa, Nana rarely spoke. She shut herself into herself and watched, her eyes as busy as a camera.

Walking to school with Ruthanne, Collie prayed that whatever was happening would somehow keep itself from happening to her.

Chapter eleven

 Sister Mary Theodora, Collie's eighth-grade nun, slapped a pile of papers on her desk. Take these down to the first grade, young lady. Hurry yourself, they're wanted. Do you hear me, girl? You've a face like a blank wall. Starin' out like that with your daydreamin,' it's a wonder you get a thing done. Now be off with yourself I said, don't be a dally. First grade. An' be sure you knock first, the sister there likes her interruptions bein' polite ones.

Yes, Sister.

Smile.

Yes Sister.

Smile.

Yes Sister Mary Gorilla.

Smile smile.

Why don't you just drop dead?

The corridors were empty. Collie knew from habit that it took four hundred thirty-nine steps and fifty-three steel-plated stairs to reach the cafeteria. The first grade was tucked behind it. Four hundred thirty-three, four hundred thirty-two. Yes, Sister. No, Sister. May I, Sister? Four hundred twenty, four hundred nineteen, four hundred purple jelly beans. Of course, Sister. Good morning, Sister. Please, Sister. Four hundred fourteen, your face is all green. Yes, Sister. Thank you, Sister.

Crunch

Thud.

Bam!

It was a nun. It was Sister Superior. She lay sprawled on the floor with her legs poking upward like unclasped safety pins. Collie's hands flew to her face in horror. She had never before seen a nun on a corridor floor, let alone one she had put there. The stunning novelty of it struck her speechless.

How many years in purgatory for knocking down a nun?

How many whacks with the ruler?

Clumsily, Collie reached to help the old nun to her feet. She might have a broken hip. Old ladies always had delicate hips. Hips were the first thing to go. Sister Superior's eyes were red and dripping. Clutching Collie, she struggled to her feet. Collie spurted apologies but to her amazement they were brushed aside.

"It's all right, child, it's all right. The fault is mine." She fluttered helplessly, a frail black bird. Blinking, she fixed her stare. Pain was lodged in her narrowed eyes; pain and something sorrowful. It poured out of her watery gray eyes and ran down her milk-white face.

"He's dead, child. Oh, He's dead!"

Collie nodded solemnly. Old people had funny ways. Here it was almost December: Jesus had been dead eight months. Shouldn't she be saying, Jesus will be born soon, child, He'll be born?

Rubbing herself, Sister Superior plodded down the hallway, choking on her own mournful sounds.

Collie pressed her face to the glass panel of the first-grade door. Instead of sitting in the usual straight rows of wooden desks, the children were in a circle of little bright plastic chairs. Their arms were waving intently. In their midst, back to the door, was a tall slender nun. Her arm was raised above her head, fingers fluttering as though she were leading a symphony through some complicated piece. She was conducting an arithmetic class.

"That's it, children. Little man. Big fat drum. Put his hat on. Once more: little man; big fat drum; put his hat on. Little man, big fat drum, put his hat on. Five. Let's all say that now: Five. Sally, don't wiggle your fingers so! Your numbers will look like a spider's web! Billy, your drum is too fat; your little man will fall over! Now let's have a parade. Here's One leading it with his marching stick. Good! Here's Two with his tuba—look how Two puffs! Here's Three in a clown suit rolling a hoop—Brian, are you feeling all right? Should you go and lie down in the office?"

The little boy Brian, achingly pale and thin, shook his head slowly from side to side. His chin trembled. Collie rapped on the glass.

"Come in!" sang out a roomful of chirpy voices.

"Come in!"

Slowly as the moon the nun turned. "Yes?" she said.

(Afterward Collie would take out that Yes? and, examining every piece of it in a thousand different lights, exclaim upon it, and clasp it to her, and slide it beneath her pillow to sleep on.) She stammered, shuffling. The papers in her hands were brick-heavy. How stupid of them not to be something pretty! She wished they were chrysanthemums.

"Sister I—I, um . . ."

Suddenly the door blew open. Spinning about, Collie caught a glimpse of Sister Superior's face—ragged, weeping, twitching out of control—and for an awful moment she expected the iron ruler to shoot out from her skirts and strike her down. Her jaw fell woodenly.

"Sister Anastasia. Sister, I've come to tell you. Oh Sister He's dead!"

Deep within herself Collie breathed a long sigh of relief.

Sister Anastasia. Anastasia. A slow breathy murmur of a name. A name that drifted like the fragrance of a lilac bush in a summer-night breeze. Anastasia, the sound made sinking into a tub full of warm soapy water. Anastasia, the sound of a Russian princess on Easter morning opening her new jeweled gold egg.

Sister Mary Anastasia looked up. "What is it, Sister?" said Sister Mary Anastasia. "Whatever has happened?"

"Our President, Sister. Mr. John Fitzgerald Kennedy. He's been shot! He's dead!" And clutching her grief with trembling bony fingers, Sister Superior rushed out.

In the din of children's wailing, children's fright because they'd never seen a nun with anything on her face but composure or displeasure, the ragged weeping and the twitching of Sister Superior's face had somehow transferred itself to the skinny little boy called Brian. He slithered to the floor and lay there, flopping about like a fish. Marbles gone into a hole, his eyes rolled back and the pupils vanished. His tongue leaped once in the air, folded itself neatly in half, and dived with a gasp into his throat. In an instant Sister Mary Anastasia was upon him. She wrapped an arm round the boy's head to hold it still while she probed to unlock his mouth. A ring of small breathless children formed around them.

"Last time he almost chewed up h'sown tongue," whispered one very blond girl.

"He gonna die too," whispered another.

Collie watched spellbound as Sister Mary Anastasia's fingers unclenched the jaws and pried open the lips.

"If she puts in her fingers Brian'll bite 'em off," said the blond girl astutely. "He won't mean to, y'know. It'll be the fit doin' it, not him."

"It's the devil, ain't it?"

"Naw."

"Is."

"Ain't."

"Is too." A terrified boy put his thumb in his mouth and sucked voraciously. Someone whimpered. Someone moaned. They all stirred restlessly.

"Be quiet, children!" commanded Collie, startling herself. Looking about, she noticed that she was the second-largest person in the room. "Hush or you'll kill him for sure!"

They hushed. Sister Mary Anastasia reached down the

side of her habit and pulled up the silver cross that dangled from the tip of her rosary. It slid easily between the boy's white lips. Collie saw her shoulders slump, saw what she took to be a prayer escape on the sigh she was breathing.

"She done that to dribe out the debil."

"Oh hush I said!"

Ever so gently Sister Mary Anastasia lifted the child. His head disappeared beneath the crisp white plate of her bib. Collie sprang to open the door.

"You'll stay with my class, won't you?" said Sister Mary Anastasia, pressing the limp body to herself. "Calm them, poor dears, keep them quiet."

"Yes, Sister," she answered gratefully. Yes Sister, yes Sister, yes! She clamped her hands to the sides of her skirt; taking a deep breath, she turned to the class and told them to sit down in their seats, or else. The clear rich sound of her own voice rang in her ears like music as twenty first-graders rushed to obey her.

On the television screen Jacqueline Kennedy, face veiled beneath her little black pillbox of a hat, held the hands of her children and mounted the steps of a vast crowded building. People parted to let them pass. Bells were tolling. "You'll stay with my class, won't you?" whispered Jacqueline Kennedy to Caroline. "Calm them, poor dears." Beside Collie, her mother was sobbing; her father's face was taut and gray. It's a sad day for our country, he repeated; a sad, sad day.

"Hush. Will you hush? I'm trying to listen," said Collie

anxiously as Jacqueline Kennedy bent closer to Caroline's ear. "Poor dears, keep them quiet," she was saying.

They'd put it on page one, there on the front page of the newspaper for the whole town to see. A thick black border surrounded it.

> *The Funeral of Our President*
> *by Colleen Elena Dutton*
>
> *My, how the tears flowed in rivers,*
> *When J.F.K. was laid in his grave.*
> *But all she showed were her shivers,*
> *For she knew he'd want her to be brave.*
>
> *From north and south and east and west,*
> *People wished J.F.K. were not dead.*
> *But Jacqueline, who loved him best,*
> *Did her crying inside of her head.*

Spreading the paper on the table as though she were laying an altar, Clare said how lovely it was; how proud they all were; how first thing in the morning she'd buy a scrapbook at the five-and-dime and paste it in. Martin shook her hand like a grownup. Congratulations on your first paycheck, he said proudly. May you have many more, and often! Mary squealed: Think of all the Hershey Kisses five dollars could buy! No, Colleen would get herself something pretty, said Clare. Besides, Christmas was coming. What a sad thing to have happen with Christmas coming, God rest his soul. He was a great man. It was a sad poem, but a good one. It was lovely. Well what have you got to say for yourself, Colleen?

Smiling to herself, Collie shrugged. Her mother said what a good thing it was for a girl to be modest. But she was not thinking of modesty. She was thinking how many chrysanthemums five dollars could buy, and what she would write on the card. She could not make up her mind whether to send them to the school or the convent, but was sure that Sister Mary Anastasia—the name was never far from her lips—would put them in a white vase on her desk and say to her class, "These are from our friend Colleen. Aren't they pretty, and so expensive in the winter!" Each time she went there to clean the boards or help correct the children's papers or write little poems to make Sister Mary Anastasia smile, she would see them, and gulp down their smell.

Chapter twelve

"The Snow Princess"

 Once upon a time a Princess with a new red shovel played in the snow outside her castle. From head to toe she was covered in fur as white as the snow, and as soft. She loved snow. She was happy to be living in a land where it snowed all the time. The day she got her new red shovel from her grandmother the Queen, she ran outside to build something out of snow. Her grandmother the Queen moved her throne close to the window so she could watch her. "Look, Grandmother, look!" called the Princess as she started building. She wanted to make a castle of snow exactly like the one she lived in. She wanted to build it just right and pour water over it to make it freeze. Then she could come out of the big castle and play in the little castle. It was a fine idea, she thought as she went to work.

She was only a little Princess, and though she had made snowmen and small houses before out of snow, she had no idea how to turn a heap of snow into a castle. She dug and dug. She scraped and patted. She pretended the snow was clay, for inside the big castle she played with clay all the time and made bowls and tiny tea cups for her grandmother the Queen. She took snow into her hands and shaped it like clay, but it didn't act like clay, and crumpled. After a whole morning the heap of snow looked like a heap of snow, not a castle. In the window her grandmother the Queen, who was old and liked her nap every day, put her head to the side and went to sleep. When Grandmother wakes up, my castle will be all finished, thought the Princess. How surprised she'll be! So she set to work again. She dug and dug. She scraped and patted. She pretended the snow was flour and water, and kneaded it as though she were baking bread. She helped her grandmother the Queen make bread all the time. It wasn't hard to roll the bread dough into fat round loaves of bread. She rolled the snow that way, but the snow wasn't bread dough. It wouldn't stick together. It wouldn't look anything like a little castle. By now the sun was high in the sky. Her fingers burned with the cold. Soon her grandmother the Queen would awaken and see nothing but a heap of snow outside. The Princess became very sad. She knew if she started to cry her tears would freeze on her face, for in that country the people only cried indoors. She pressed her eyes together, but the tears spilled out anyway.

Suddenly there was a rustle in the bushes that separated the castle from the hunting grounds where her grandfather the King rode horses. The Princess thought it must be rabbits, and went on crying. A voice came out of the bushes. "Why are you crying, little Princess?" said the voice. The

Princess had heard many tales in which rabbits talk, and thought this must be one of them. But it wasn't a rabbit. It was a little man. It was a funny little man with pointed shoes and a long white beard that went to his knees. Then there was another one, and another one. Three funny little men, all dressed the same, all with white beards that seemed to be made of the snow. How did they get their beards like that, thought the Princess, when I can't make snow do what I want and be a castle? The three funny little men came out of the bushes and stood around her, looking at her with big dark eyes. They were nice eyes. "Why are you crying?" they said. "Don't cry, or you'll have icicles all over your face." The Princess told the three funny little men how the snow wouldn't turn into a castle, and any minute her grandmother the Queen would awaken. How disappointed her grandmother the Queen would be to look out the window and see nothing but a heap of snow where the little snow castle ought to be! And the princess put her fur-covered hands to her eyes and went on crying. One of the funny little men touched her arm. She felt something warm pass through her. She felt as though she had swallowed a mugful of steamy chocolate. It was nice. "Don't cry," said the funny little man. "We'll help you." Then the three little men did something magic. They said some words she'd never heard before, but they were nice words. They sounded like the tinkle of bells on her grandfather the King's horses as they pulled a sled over the sparkling white snow. They sounded like her puppy's breath when it curled up on her knees in front of the fire. They sounded like the soft cackle and hiss of the fire logs breaking into ashes and smoke. The Princess closed her eyes and filled herself with those words, forgetting all about the heap of snow and her grandmother the Queen sleeping at the window. Suddenly the words sounded like the snow itself, and when she opened her eyes the three little men had vanished. In their place was a castle already frozen hard. It had rooms and a drawbridge. It had peaks and spires. It had a throne close to the window for her grandmother the sleeping Queen. At the top of the castle was her new red shovel, stuck on the highest spire like a flag. "Oh!" the Princess exclaimed. "Oh, it's just what I wanted!" She looked around for the three funny little men, to thank them. She looked and looked, poking through the bushes on her hands and knees, but all she saw were three little white rabbits, soft and white as the snow. But there was her castle. It was just her size. And there was her grandmother the Queen, nodding her head at the window. "Look, Grandmother, look!" called the Princess. "See what I made for you!" And with a big smile her grandmother the Queen looked at the castle made of snow, and though the Princess couldn't hear the words, she knew her grandmother the Queen was saying how good it was, how pretty.

This is the end of a story by Colleen Elena Dutton, which was written for Sister Mary Anastasia's first-grade class.

When she finished reading, Sister Mary Anastasia smoothed the pages on top of her desk. For a long moment she said nothing, her pale white hand hovering over the story as if it were trying to decide what to do with it. Toss it in the trash? Set it on fire? Collie silently groaned, squirming with her knees bent nearly to her chin in the little plastic first-grade chair. She knew she was sitting there waiting for judgment, but she couldn't bring herself to look. She cast her eyes on the clock, the low chalkboard, the familiar alphabet pictures arranged on the walls. She had been the one to help Sister Mary Anastasia cut those pictures from magazines. It had taken an entire Saturday afternoon. Apple, airplane. Bambi, bicycle. Carrots, cheese. She had them memorized. Donald Duck, Lassie. She had pasted them onto construction paper, and tacked them onto the wall while she stood on Sister Mary Anastasia's chair and Sister Mary Anastasia, holding the chair in place, told her what it felt like to ride a horse alone through a field in western Connecticut. She had had a horse of her own, a shocking but wonderful thing for a nun. But she'd been a girl then. The horse's name was Dancer.

Elephant, frog, goose, house, igloo, Jesus, kite. Sister Mary Anastasia lifted the pages of the story and held it up with the same kind of care Collie had often seen her take with the Bible. Sister Mary Anastasia cleared her throat. Collie flushed, her face burning. She found it difficult to get her breath.

"It's an excellent story, Colleen," said Sister Mary Anastasia. "Hurry and write something else!"

Sister Mary Anastasia's proud smile went through Collie like sunshine. Rushing home, she spent the rest of the day in her room, and when she came out again she went running to her father for a stamp to send her brand-new poem to the newspaper.

The Summer Sun
by Colleen Elena Dutton

Orange and yellow and golden and red,
Summertime sneaks in this time every year.
The sun comes so close it touches your head
With halos of flame, but nothing to fear.
School's out for the summer. The children play.
And the sun it gets warmer every day.

"Hmmf," said Clare, frowning over the newspaper. "I don't think the ending's quite right. You'd expect there to be more. Is this all of it, Colleen? You're sure they didn't leave some out? If they left some out you might not get all the five dollars."

"Don't you think she'd know if they left something out of her own poem?" said Martin. "I think it's fine the way it is."

"Me too," said Mary, twirling a basketball on her fingers. She'd just learned how.

"All the same there's something about it—maybe the halos of flame. Colleen, why in the world did you say halos of flame?"

"I think she means sunlight," said Martin. "Do you mean sunlight, Colleen?"

"Sure she means sunlight," said Mary dropping her ball. "It's round and yellow, ain't it?"

"A flame may be yellow, but sure as I'm sitting here no flame is round."

"Oh Mother, do you have to be so picky? She can write a poem how she likes. It's a free country, ain't it?"

"Well if she means sunlight, why not say sunlight. Why

not call a thing what it is and be done with it? Colleen, why don't you call a thing what it is? Well? What have you to say for yourself?"

Collie shrugged and went on laying the table for dinner. She had said it was excellent. Not good, not anything else, but *excellent*. She said she'd keep the story forever. Not only until eighth grade was over and it would be time to go, but *forever*.

All through supper she kept chewing on those words: excellent and forever.

 1964

Chapter thirteen

Pulling the bathtub plug, she was a Coronation girl. Stepping out, she wrapped a towel round her Coronation self. She shook out her Coronation hair. Running a comb through it, she untangled a Coronation snarl. Hurry up in there, will you, said Mary, thumping on the door in a way not fit for Coronation ears. Hurry, it's nearly time, called her mother, holding out the Coronation blouse and jumper. Each pleat creased perfectly, fold upon fold of rich deep blue wool, and slipping into it, Collie felt every part of her being rise in tremulous joy. The skirt fell to the center of her knees in a delicious soft caress. I am a Coronation girl, I am, I am, she thought for the hundredth time. A Coronation girl am I. The word sat like a chocolate drop on her tongue. She sucked it and rubbed it against her lips and felt it flow through her body. Lifting a cup at the breakfast table, she caught a glimpse of a Coronation face: Why that's me, she thought excitedly, and could not bring herself to drink. Fear and exaltation numbed and bewitched her. She could not sit still; she could not move.

Don't you dare slouch, young lady, said Clare, lifting the Coronation jacket with the little *O*, big *C*, little *L* sewn over the pocket.

Coronation girls don't slouch. Imagine you are walking with a book on your head.

A Coronation girl is clean in thought and word and deed.

A Coronation girl is pure in mind and body and heart and soul.

She is the flower of youth, the unblemished rose in the garden of Life. Not every girl is so lucky.

Did you brush your teeth, young lady?

For heaven's sake, Colleen, stand up straight. You're a Coronation girl!

The day you walk through the doors of Our Lady of the Coronation High is the proudest most significant day of your life (said the sister on Orientation Day). You have proven the superior abilities of your minds in the examinations. I know that for most of you it was a tremendously harrowing experience, as the exams are painfully long and demanding, but you've come through with flying colors. (Here Collie couldn't help a quick sidelong glance at Ruthanne, who had failed the examinations, but since it was her father's concrete in the foundation of Our Lady of the Coronation she'd got in. Nobody knew but Collie.) Let me say, girls—or, as you will henceforward be addressed, young ladies—let me say, young ladies, that as you enter Our Lady of the Coronation your minds are like damp fertile earth tilled by loving hands and ready to be sown with seeds that will bring forth a plentiful harvest. It is our responsibility to plant those seeds and nurture their growth, and we shall do so in the great and sacred tradition of our school. Gone is the waywardness of your childish ways! In its place is the budding maturity of young ladies who have disdained the vulgarity of the public school in favor of the select community of the scholar, the maiden of the Lord, the noble caretaker of the flame of knowledge instilled in our breast by Our Most Holy Mother—welcome, ladies, oh welcome to our school!

Tie your laces, said Clare. Won't do to have you tripping on your own feet. For the love of God, Colleen, stand up straight!

Knees knocking, she climbed the steps of the Coronation bus and sank into a window seat near the front. Ruthanne slid in after her, eyes rolling crazily. From all sides girls were chattering, fluttering, squirming. Collie recognized several faces, but nobody looked the same. Ruthanne pressed her hand as the bus lurched off.

Goodbye, Colleen, goodbye! Her mother and father and sister waved from the front porch. The porch needed paint. The steps were sagging shamefully.

Goodbye, Colleen! How ordinary they looked, how plain. Her father's briefcase was coming apart at the seams. Her mother's old housedress flopped in the breeze like a rag. There was jelly all over her sister's face. Collie turned from the window as if that family belonged to somebody else.

A Coronation girl is the pride of her community. She is

the gift of the past, the promise of the present, the hope of the future. In the mighty river of Life, she swims against the tides of temptation. She is strong as an anchor when other girls flounder and drown. As long as she wears the crest of the Coronation, she need fear no untimely demise.

"Aren't you nervous," whispered Ruthanne, giddily clasping and unclasping her fingers. "Aren't you scared?"

The bus lunged down the familiar sweep of the hill. They passed the maples with their first signs of autumn color and house after house where children in new shoes bounced on porches, waiting for their friends. They passed the gas station and the offices of Arthur J. Bent, General Contractor. (Oh there's Daddy, squealed Ruthanne. Why won't you wave to Daddy, Colleen?) They passed the five-and-dime and the fire station, where denim-shirted firemen sat on lawn chairs waiting for the schoolchildren to appear, for they had licorice sticks in honor of first day. They passed the church and Jake's Grille, and Jake himself paused in the sweeping of his sidewalk to shake his broom in greeting. They approached the grammar school, where early children were romping, and Collie eagerly perched at the edge of her seat. (To think we once were children here, sighed Ruthanne smugly.) She pressed her face to the glass. She'd said she'd be here. She'd promised. She'd said she'd be standing near the front door even if it was an hour till class. The bus crept past, past girls hopscotching and boys playing kickball. Just as the school slid from view a dark arm shot out of the doorway, signaling like a flag. The familiar face beneath it was beaming. "Oh look," whinnied Ruthanne. "Isn't that Sister Mary Anastasia?"

"Goodbye, Collie," came the thrilling voice of Sister Mary Anastasia. "Good luck!" Collie waved, feeling proud and happy. She was a Coronation girl. It was what she'd always wanted to be.

The seniors formed a solid thick wall of unfriendly faces. They loafed in the yard, leaned in the doorway, squatted on the lawn. They were armed with large books, pointed pencils, nailfiles, and pocketknives that bulged beneath the little *O*, big *C*, little *L* of their blazer shields. Many wore chrome barrettes in their hair or gold rings large enough to put an eye out. It was impossible to get to the front door without confronting them.

"Oooh, they're so big," uttered Ruthanne under her breath as the girls entered the yard. Slowly, gingerly, they crept down the narrow winding path beneath the reassuring rustle of elm leaves. They were huge, magnificent trees staunchly rooted in place; their roots stretched for yards, meeting and entwining each other in a vast network of safety and good sense. The trunks were too wide to get a pair of arms around, but two strong legs could shinny up, and—Collie gasped. There was a senior in a tree, grinning down at her like a cat.

"Hey, freshman, did jer mother change yer diapers 'fore ya left? Whatsamatta? Scaredy-pants?"

"I don't like this," whispered Ruthanne, clutching her arm. "I don't like this one bit, Colleen. I want to go home."

"Hush, Ruthie, pretend they're invisible."

On they walked, feet crunching on the gravel path, hearts thumping wildly.

"Hey will ya look at that one, Maureen? That one got a mouthful o' steel—hey metal-mouth!"

"Ooh lookey here, this one got brand-new shoes—hey squeaky-feet!"

"Sylvia, I do say, isn't this the scrawniest bunch o' freshmen you ever did see? Where'd ya come from girls, kindagadden?"

"Hey freshies, didja ever git french-kissed?"

"Ha, can you 'magine kissin' that one? She's so ugly yer tongue'd turn black!"

"Oh lookit the one with the freckles! Whatsamatta, polka dots, didn't ya get born finished?"

More giggles. Ruthanne turned crimson and quivered.

"You went an' hurt polka dots, Marylou, you crumb. Now she's turnin' red!"

"Say somethin' else make her turn green, I want to see her green!"

"That reminds me of a joke. Hey freshies, you like jokes? What's red and green and goes a hundred miles a minute?"

"I give up, what?"

"A frog in an electric mixer!"

"There she goes, Marylou—oooh she's green all over!"

"I want to go home, Colleen, I don't like this at all," sniffed Ruthanne.

The bell. Mercifully the bell rang and, as though cued to walk onstage, the seniors snapped to attention, smoothed out their skirts, gathered up their books, patted their hair, and proceeded gracefully into the building.

"Come on, Ruthie, we'll be late."

"I don't like it here. I want to go home."

"Oh, don't be a prissface, Ruthanne, come on." Collie gave her a sharp tug and pushed her through the door.

"Welcome, dear freshmen, to Our Lady of the Coronation," cooed the senior they'd called Maureen. She was positioned inches beyond the door, her hands cupped like a hostess waiting to take their umbrellas. Her voice was sugary sweet. "Step right this way, ladies, and straight ahead to Hall. Assembly begins in four minutes."

"There," whispered Collie. "Everything's all right. Will you stop that, Ruthie. Everyone will think you're a priss."

"I don't like it here. I don't like it here at all."

"Ruthanne Bent, if you don't cut that out I will tell everyone in this school you flunked the entrance exam."

"You wouldn't!"

"I would too." Collie pulled her face into a grim hard expression and crooked her arms to her hips. Ruthanne's nose was twiching like a rabbit's, a sure sign that tears were coming. Her lower lip puckered. Her eyes filled.

"Ruthie—stop it right now. Ruthie, you better not cry. Aw, Ruthie, please don't cry."

"You would do that?"

"No. I wouldn't. Honest. I just said it so you'd cut out pouting."

"Colleen?"

"Yeah, Ruthie."

"We'll still be best friends?"

"Yeah."

"Honest to God cross your heart hope to die?"

"Yeah."

"Well say it, Colleen. Say it."

Collie looked away at the groups of girls disappearing into Hall. "Crossmyheartanhopetodie," she said quickly. "Come on."

They slid into the last row of seats as a guitar began its first tentative twangs. Collie looked around at a sea of Coronation jackets topped by head after head held straight and high. The Hall was a large high-ceilinged room, windowless yet airy. Oak panels covered most of the walls that weren't covered with life-size portraits of popes and bishops and nuns, all stern and unsmiling. Up on the stage, where the deep red curtains had been drawn to reveal a backdrop of whitewashed canvas, sat the faculty. Thirty nuns. Nuns looking bemused, attentive, somber, mean, friendly, harsh, tyrannical. Thin nuns and haggard nuns. Corpulent nuns and red-cheeked nuns. Spectacled nuns and heavy-lidded nuns. A nun with a nose like a knitting hook. A nun with front teeth like a beaver's. A nun with freckles. Ruthanne relaxed beside her. The guitars were tuned and ready: below the stage, seniors were bending in a circle over their instruments like angels with harps. The singing began: a clear strong song that sent three hundred bodies swaying. The sounds bounced off the oak walls, brought laughter to the lips of the popes and bishops, and reverberated in a joyous swirl of united cheer. Girls looked at each other and smiled toothily. Nuns on the stage threw back their heads in a collective flinging of veils and sang with their mouths wide open.

So this, thought Collie as the music mounted and soared, is what it means to be a Coronation girl. This is it. Sensing her thoughts, the guitars picked them up like leaves and carried them off. The swelling in her own throat and the swelling of the music, the words, the girls, the nuns, were one and the same.

One of the guitarists called out an order for everyone to salute a stranger. The room was a flurry of giggles and exclamations. Nuns bowed to the audience. The audience bowed to the nuns. Girls sat at the edges of their chairs and tapped each other on the fingers. Hello! Hello! they tweeted. A broad-shouldered body in front of Collie turned around, and Collie recognized the senior called Marylou. Ruthanne shuddered.

"Hi, freshmen," said Marylou with a big smile.

"Hi," echoed Collie and Ruthanne. Breaking loose, the guitars skidded into a brisker rhythm and caught the wake of the thunderous sound of hands clapping and feet stomping the old wood floor. Collie slid into the feeling of being part of something big and wonderful and happy. She stole a sidelong glance at Ruthanne, her dearest friend Ruthanne with the shimmery eyes, and sent her an unstoppable grin. Ruthanne's hand closed round Collie's as though they were about to take a plunge on a ferris wheel.

"Hey! What's this?"

A rough gruff voice slashed through the music, the clapping, the stomping. Marylou spun angrily around. At once the music halted. At once every breath in the room was sucked in and held. Ruthanne blanched, her fingers in Collie's tight as wire.

"Look at these two, willya? What are you anyway, lezzies? I'm not gonna sit near any lezzies—oh no!" As though her seat had suddenly caught fire, Marylou sprang to her feet. Upheaved, all the other girls squirmed in confusion. Nuns came off the stage like bowling pins. Ruthanne burst into tears and flung herself across Collie's shoulders. Collie froze. She dared not touch her.

Like the single, piercing cry of a trumpet that hurdles over an orchestra on a flight so high it leaves the ears dazzled, the word stayed. *Lezzies.* It hardened and hurt. It crawled under her skin and burrowed deeper and deeper until she wanted to fling herself out the window just to be rid of it. With the word came an image: Marylou's face in an ugly sneer, teeth bared, glinting white-hot fury. It was the face she had seen before on the men in her neighborhood who pulled back their lips to say *those spicks.* It was the face in the newspaper when children and grownups taunted the girl she'd named Amanda on her way to school. It was the face of Jake Trombley every time he said *damn the commies.* It was the face that haunted her dreams and half-sleeps when, running and stumbling, she tried to flee it, begging for help: the face saying awful things, things you would surely go to hell for saying. There was a face an ugly face, there were three faces hiding in the bushes. It was winter. Nana stood watching in the window, Nana with her sore legs that tottered like towers made of building blocks. For days the lines in her face had sagged and frozen. She was cold all the time. Her skin turned as yellow as the cheese she bought at the grocer's. Bloodless, her lips forgot how to smile. Old women came in and out of the house, hiding their faces under black capes that fell to their ankles in wide pleating folds. Collie wanted to stop them and cover herself with their clothing, and hide from the grim yellow stare that covered up Nana like a mask. Nana stood watching at the window even though the aunts had told her not to. Clare talked to Nana like a mother: Come away from that window, you'll catch a draft. Nana said in Italian, How lovely the snow is: not even a bride has a thing so white! Go outside, child, and make me a statue of snow. Make something nice for your Nana.

It was a brand-new shovel, silver and red. She dug, flinging snow in the air, catching some on her tongue. It was crazy with cold. At the window Nana pressed her face to the glass, watching. Look, Nana, at what I'm making for you! There was a rustle in the bushes, the bushes crouching under ice and snow. A face appeared. Another. Another. Faces bleating, faces twisted, strange faces spitting words that came hurling over the snow like rocks.

Hey garlic breath!

Hey wop!

Hey you greasy guinea! Spitting, the faces came closer. She arched like a cat. Her gloved fingers closed around the handle of her new red and silver shovel. In the window Nana watched, the makings of a smile hovering at the ends of her mouth.

Nie nie nie wop wop wop.

All the time there was the face in the window, the face that was begging for something pretty in the snow. Don't you say things like that or my Nana will take Grandpapa's strap to you!

Greasy dirty guinea we don't want nobody here like you.

Nana waved. Her mouth moved. Are you having a good time, dear?

Closer they came. She could almost smell the hatred on their breaths. She felt her own breath catch in her throat and the odd thrilling surge of danger.

Heyyougreasywopyermotherfuckswithsausagesyouknow-whatwelldotoyou?

Up went her shovel like the stroke of a sword. A faint whistling filled her ears. She struck. One, two, three times, she struck against one face, and the other faces dissolved back into the frozen bushes where they had come from. The face she hit wasn't hard at all but still she went on hitting. The face she hit was soft, soft and crumbling, soft and melting, soft as the snow, soft and spilling blood that ate through the snow like liquid fire. She turned around quickly toward the house. Soft was the face in the window. Soft and white and icy. Down it fell. Collie leaped over the body of the boy on the ground and flung herself through the back door.

She had fallen, clutching the table leg by the window. She lay there in a heap, opening her mouth to speak, but no words came though she tried and tried. Yet there was her mouth opening and closing, there was her gold tooth like an expensively wrapped candy. Her bony protruding jaws snapped open and shut as foamy splotches trickled out the edges of her very white and silent mouth. Her eyes opened wide and glassy and stayed that way. Their horrible blankness was trying to burn holes into Collie's flesh.

The scream she screamed brought the aunts and her

mother running. She pressed her fingers against her eyelids as if her own eyes had told her a lie. The scream kept on coming. But no matter how hard she shut her eyes, the mouth was there opening and closing, as if it meant to swallow her whole. Then the world dissolved into blackness, and all was still.

It was a stroke, the doctor said in English, buttoning up his topcoat in Nana's kitchen. He must have said it in English, or how else would she have understood?

Stepping over each other, the aunts boiled water for tea. Grandpapa came home and disappeared upstairs. Clare was crying. The old Italian women came in a procession through the kitchen, muttering like drums. They lit red candles across the mantelpiece in the living room. They left their black capes in a heap on Nana's rocking chair. Collie stayed out of their way. In the doorway the doctor paused and held out his hand to the aunts. It was a stroke, he told them.

How could he have known? In a corner of the kitchen Collie rocked back and forth on her heels. There was no stopping the trembling of her whole body. She shivered and rocked against the hard large thing deep inside her that seemed to grow bigger and bigger. It was something that wanted to reach all the way to her heart and squeeze it dry. It was a stroke: of course it was a stroke; it was the stroke of her red and silver shovel. The doctor put his hand to the door and said, as if in afterthought, "There've been some boys fighting in your yard. One of them got messed up a little and we've put him in the hospital. Nothing to worry about."

The women didn't pay any attention to him. He shook his head sadly and went out into the cold, closing the door behind him. He knew. He knew but he wasn't going to tell on her.

She sat in the corner, praying into her hands that no one else would ever find out.

Mr. Bent's long silver Buick was parked outside the school. Leaning against the window in the chemistry lab, Collie idly traced the little *O*, big *C*, little *L* on the pocket of her new uniform. The elm trees were busily genuflecting. Sky to earth, sky to earth, they seemed like long comfortable arms swaying in time to music. She thought if she could only slip outside and press herself to an elm tree, and cover her face with its leaves, she might hear what the trees heard, and understand it, and stop the ache that was throbbing away inside her. She had never been in a chemistry lab before. It smelled cold. It smelled like a room in a hospital. She turned her back on the rows of sinks, where generations of Coronation girls had turned on the taps, heads bent over their experiments. She imagined their giggles, these ghosts; she imagined a roomful of girls in uniforms just like her own, all tittering into their fingers over the spectacle Ruthanne Bent had caused that morning at assembly.

"I'm a Coronation girl, I *am*," she said to herself for the hundredth time.

"C-Colleen?"

She spun, startled. Ruthanne was standing in the door-way. She was biting her lower lip and her shoulders were twitching oddly. She'd been crying hard and was about to cry even harder. Collie's first impulse was to run to her holding out her arms.

"I-I'm getting out of here, Colleen. Aren't you going to—?"

A look Collie knew by now came into Ruthanne's face. The corners of her mouth turned up tightly and her red-dened eyes seemed to grow dull. She gave herself a little shake and sent the skirt of her uniform rippling. Her voice thinned into a whine. "Aren't you coming with me? Daddy's here with the car."

Collie couldn't bring herself to look Ruthanne in the eye.

"Well, Colleen?" Ruthanne stamped her foot impa-tiently. "What are you waiting for? Come *on!*"

Up bubbled images like a speeded-up movie. Ruthanne and her gently rolling eyes underneath the pine trees. Ruth-anne passing notes under the desk tops. Ruthanne in her white silky gown on Confirmation night, sad and sorry Ruthanne, who never knew what had really happened. Ruthanne the prissface, who had told the whole school Martin Dutton was a Communist. Ruthanne, the girl who had caused a hurt so bad that somewhere deep inside of Collie there would always be a place still aching over Ruth-anne Bent. In the back of her mind Collie remembered her mother saying how she never could quite see what some-body like Collie could see in somebody like Ruthie Bent and with all the girls in town how could Collie ever pick a best friend like Ruthie—not that Ruthie was *bad*, Clare had said. Ruthie was, well, Ruthie. And with that memory came the sight of Ruthanne in her little skating skirt, showing up at the river like an alien being, calling herself a lady. All over again Ruthie wanted her to do something she knew for sure she couldn't do. Collie blinked rapidly.

"I'm a Coronation girl," she said finally. "If you want to go to another school, I can't stop you." Her voice was flat and heavy and low. There wasn't a single thing to be said. But Ruthanne went on standing in the doorway clutching her new books, as if she were hard at work thinking up some new thing to make Collie change her mind. Just then a bell rang out in the hallway. It was nearly time for chemistry class. Her first chemistry class. Ruthanne threw a wild look out the door, but before she could say anything more Collie took a step forward, crossed her arms over her chest, and let her voice sound as chilly as she could possibly make it.

"Don't look at me like that, Ruthie, like you're about to cry for a week. You want to go? Well I don't. It's as easy as that, isn't it?"

She watched for the hard words to hit home, watched without moving or changing her expression as a crumpled, hurt look appeared in Ruthanne's eyes and spread real as water all over her body. Collie turned back to the window, bracing herself for Ruthanne's outburst. Nothing happened. The elm trees were silently swaying, tossing back their leaves like a woman's hair. Behind Collie, the girls in the chemistry class were coming in bunches through the door. In a moment she would turn and face them. But now, down in the street, Mr. Bent was heading for the Buick with Ruthie huddled close beside him. He unlocked the door and helped her inside. Going round to the driver's side, he kept his eyes off Our Lady of Coronation High as if it simply did not exist.

The engine turned. The car rolled away and vanished.

Collie took a deep breath. Woodenly, she went to find her seat, picking her way through the other girls, the Coronation girls. Some of them looked up as she passed, and smiled.

"Poor Ruthie," said Clare that night at supper. "Imagine getting sick on the first day of school. All the same, I always thought that girl was a weak one. I hear they'll be sending her to that school over in Lowell, that little school that's been there only about a year. It's just as well. I never thought all that much would come of her. She's a Bent, after all. Never were much brains in the Bents. Mind, there's nothing wrong with Ruthie. It's just that I never did think she'd turn out to be a Coronation girl. Hold out your plate, Colleen. You're awfully quiet tonight. Well, how was it? Did you have a good day your first day?"

"Yes," she replied. "Yes. Pass the salt, will you?"

 1965

Chapter fourteen

She had just turned fifteen and the sky was a riot of stars running into each other like milk spilled across a blackness that had no beginning, no end. In her room she opened the window and let the chilly night come inside. There was a moon peeking through the black trees, a scarred, blazing moon. She tilted her head on the windowsill, wondering how hard it would be to get down on paper the exact yellow, the just-right glare, the halo-like glow that made her think the moon was pumping its heart out only for her and her pen. She reached for some paper. Nothing happened except a sudden sharp pounding on the door.

"Come in, Mother," she said with weariness. "The door's not locked."

Clare sat down on the bed. "Doing your homework, Colleen?"

"I was, until you came." Although the sheet of paper

was blank, she swept it under a pile of books. "I've been doing Latin."

Clare clucked but quickly became serious. "I spent half the day looking for you, Colleen. Where were you?"

Collie rolled her eyes to the ceiling with a shrug. "Out."

"Were you at Ruthie's? I tried calling there."

"No. Don't you know anything, Mother? I *never* go to Ruthie's anymore."

"Were you with Sister Anastasia? Mary said she thought you might be there, helping Sister decorate her classroom."

"Of course I wasn't."

"Well, didn't Sister send you a note, asking you to come by?"

"Maybe she did, but what's the difference? I'm fifteen, Mother. I'm too old for that crap."

"Colleen! Colleen Dutton, don't you dare—"

"Stuff. I'm sorry. I just mean that—oh, never mind what I mean. Come and look at the moon, Mother. Isn't it lovely?"

Clare stretched forward, muttering as she looked out the window, "Don't you go trying to change the topic, Colleen, getting me mushy over your moon. I want to know what you've been up to, gone all day without telling anyone where you're off to. It's not right for a girl your age. My though, isn't that a pretty one! So yellow tonight!"

Collie blushed, as if she were being praised for something she herself had just made.

"If I were you, Colleen, I'd write a nice poem about that moon. You know what I mean. The moon in June. A pretty tune." Clare's voice trailed off dreamily.

"It's not June, Mother." Collie scrunched her lips as though she'd just swallowed something sour.

"Well, you get the meaning. I like them better when they rhyme." Clare, remembering what she had come for, sat back on the bed, folding her arms across her chest. "Now, young lady, where have you been off to?"

"Nowhere. I told you. Nowhere."

Clare brightened with anger. "Now you listen to me, Colleen. You're not so big I can't walk out of here and shut the door behind me and tell you you're not to come out of this room until I say so. You got that?"

Collie looked at the wall.

"Answer me!"

"Do what you like, Mother," she said indifferently. A very large part of her wanted to run to her mother and fling herself into Clare's arms. Instead, she went on staring at the wall as Clare tore out, slamming the door behind her. Collie rose and locked it, imagining how Clare would go straight out of her mind if she knew the truth.

It's like this, Mother, Collie thought: I spent the whole day at the cemetery. I just can't believe they went and did it. Those trees! Those wonderful trees!

Hmmf, Clare would say. What kind of a girl are you anyway, spending your free time around people's *graves*. What'll people say?

But the pine trees had come down.

She had watched the ground harden and close in the empty places where they had been. Even the roots were gone. A new metal fence went up, harsh and gleaming, impossible to climb. The gates of the fence shut at twilight.

Two German shepherds, with teeth as long as the spikes at the top of the fence, stood inside the gates every night, foaming and growling. All over town people said how sad it was that they had come to that: guard dogs at the cemetery. But they all agreed it was a necessary thing. Nobody ever mentioned the pines. In the spring the gravediggers dug graves as though nothing else had ever lived there. Faster and faster things were changing, and none of it was fair.

She went back to her poem about the moon. As her mind worked over the words *yellow*, *blazing*, *halo*, she wondered what Ruthanne would do if she wrote her a very short note.

Dear Ruthie, she would say, I hope things are going well for you at your school. Do you ever think about me?

Dear Ruthie, Mary told me that she saw you last week with a boy from Lowell and he's got about a million pimples all over his face. I hope you are having a happy time.

Dear Ruthie, I just want to let you know that when they went to bulldoze down the pine trees at the cemetery I tried to stop them by throwing myself under the blades but seven men with axes got me out of the way and held me down. Well, not really held me down. But they said they'd call my mother if I didn't go home. Do you ever miss me?

It was no good trying to write about the moon. The moon was empty and faraway, an idiot thing that stared its blank stare along with the cold pinpricks of vacant stars. But she took up her pen again, the way someone with a serious illness would take up a spoonful of medicine. She wrote as a title "If You Knew" and let the words all come as if they had a life of their own.

If you knew how I was blindly
reeling would you feeling
kindly hold your arms out
hold me tightly would you
if you felt me aching would
you help me keep from breaking
if by chance you came by walking
stop a moment for some talking
would you say, how are you, would
you if you knew how much I'm
missing would you miss me too?

The next day she walked to Ruthie's house, the poem tucked in her pocket. Ruthanne came out onto the porch to meet her. If she was surprised she didn't show it.

"Hi, Ruthie."

"Hi."

"How's school?"

"Okay. How's yours?"

"Same. You got your hair cut."

"Yeah, just the other day. Do you like it?"

"Sure. It's—it's pretty."

"Thank you." Ruthanne sat down on the porch step, tossing anxious looks toward the house.

"You're welcome. Can I sit down?"

"If you want to." Ruthanne gestured to a spot on the bottom step and Collie took it. Looking up, Collie stared hard, trying to place exactly what was making Ruthanne's face so different. "That's a pretty sweater, Colleen. It matches your eyes."

Collie scowled. "Oh it does *not*, Ruthie. Nothing goes with my eyes. I've got mousy eyes."

"No you don't." Again Ruthie was looking over her shoulder at the front door. Collie followed her eyes, expecting someone to come charging out of the house—but who?

"You've got nice eyes, Colleen," Ruthie said with the same kind of distraction people have when they talk about the weather.

"You don't have to be nice. Everyone knows I've got eyes just like a mouse's."

"Oh you do not."

"Oh I do too." And it came to Collie that Ruthanne looked different because her freckles were gone. No, not gone. Collie gasped. "You're wearing make-up on your face, Ruthie!"

Ruthanne patted the sides of her cheeks proudly. "Don't you like it?"

"I like your freckles. I—"

Ruthanne cut her off, changing the subject. "Would you like something to drink? Something hot? It's so cold out here. I could get you a cup of tea." Back and forth went Ruthie's eyes, the door to the bottom step, door to bottom step. Collie was beginning to feel dizzy.

"I hate tea, Ruthie. Don't you remember how I hate tea? Tea's what my mother always made me drink whenever I threw up."

"Oh." Ruthanne cupped her chin in her hands and sat still, reminding Collie of herself whenever she wanted to get rid of pestering Mary. Collie dug her hands into her pocket, closing her fingers around Ruthanne's poem. She couldn't think of a single thing to say.

"It was nice of you to stop by, Colleen," Ruthie said flatly. Collie jumped to her feet.

"Sure. I—I just wanted to say hello."

"Thank you. I hope you do it again real soon," said Ruthie, like a television commercial or a telephone operator. The make-up gave her a strange, make-believe look, as though her blood had been drained and all that was left was a thin coating of faintly pinkened white paste.

"Well, so long," said Collie.

"So long, Colleen."

Ruthanne stayed on the porch until Collie walked as far as the street; then quickly she dashed back into the house. Watching her go, Collie reached into her pocket and squeezed the poem into a wad. Back in her own room she tore it to shreds and buried it at the bottom of the wastebasket.

"See if I ever write you another one, Ruthanne Bent!" she cried.

 1966

Chapter fifteen

Just after the start of junior year, word went out that Sister Principal wanted to see Colleen Dutton in her office. In the hallways sympathetic girls parted like the Red Sea to let her by.

"Don't look so scared," someone said from behind the door of an open locker.

"Whatever she says, just be sorry," said someone else. "Cry if you have to. Say you'll make a novena or two."

Collie rapped on the office door and went in. "Yes, Sister?"

The tall, lean nun rose slightly from behind her big desk. Her dark eyes seemed the exact shade of her black habit, and today they were sparking like a pair of red-hot coals.

"Sit down, Colleen."

"Th-thank you, Sister." If she had had to stand one more second, her legs would have given way.

"I'm going to come straight to the point, Colleen. You have been doing exceptionally well here. All of your teachers are quick to point to your high grades, especially in your language classes. Tell me, are you happy with Our Lady of the Coronation?"

Collie nodded vigorously.

The nun's ordinarily ruddy face dropped a shade to a very pale pink. Her lips formed a single straight line. Collie tried to make herself very small in the chair as her mind sped forward trying to recall Sister Principal's favorite novenas. She would promise to say twenty novenas if it came to that.

"If you like it so much here, Colleen, why in the world have you done something like—like *this*?"

Sister Principal dropped onto her desk a wrinkled sheet of paper covered with Collie's handwriting. Her eyes narrowed in anger. Collie silently prayed a prayer to Our Lady of Perpetual Help, the only saint she could think of to get her out of this one.

The nun's voice remained calm and evenly measured. "Don't bother wondering how this—this—this *horror* came into my possession. Suffice it to say that I am deeply shocked by you, Colleen. What you have written here is not only a thing of grave offense. It is an abomination. Tell me, is this the sort of poem you would like your parents to see?"

Collie's eyes opened wide at the thought. "No, Sister." Good God!

Sister Principal held up the paper, reading it to herself for a long silent moment. Collie prayed that she could be back in Sister Mary Anastasia's cheerful first grade, with Sister Mary Anastasia looking up from one of Collie's stories, using words like *excellent.*

"What you have managed to do in one fell swoop is to turn some of the most sacred and mystical aspects of our faith into . . . into *talk of the gutter*, Colleen. Is that where you come from, the *gutter*?"

"N-no, Sister. Please, Sister, I want to say from the bottom of my heart that I am so very, very—"

The nun raised her hand to silence her. "Sorry isn't good enough, Colleen. The Good Lord has given you a talent, a remarkable one at that. And here you have seen fit to praise God with the very cheapest, very basest, most horridly vulgar words that I have ever seen a Coronation girl use. You should be ashamed of yourself."

In a very tiny voice Collie said that she was.

Sister rose and came round to the front of her desk, looking down at Collie with the paper dangling from her fingers. "Take this, and in front of me destroy it. Go ahead, tear it to pieces."

Trembling, Collie managed to rip it neatly down the center. Her hands were shaking too hard to do more.

"Now throw it away, and never allow yourself to degrade yourself or this school in such a *vile* manner. Am I making myself understood?"

Biting her lip, Collie looked up over the wastebasket. "Does . . . does this mean that I'm going to be—" The thought was too awful to say.

"Expelled?" To Collie's amazement, Sister Principal shook her head slowly from side to side. "I have something else in mind for you, Colleen." She went back to her seat. "As you may know, our all-school Dramatic isn't too far off. I think we have every reason to be proud of our theatrical tradition here, don't you?"

"Oh yes, Sister, yes!" Relief flooded every part of her.

"And as you know we like to choose dramatic works that involve as many students as possible. We also want to use the stage as a medium to reflect our lives at Coronation. You've been working with Sister on stagecraft, haven't you?"

"Yes, Sister," she answered, feeling confused. "Last year I was assistant stage manager."

"I remember. You did a fine job. But this year things will be a bit different. We have joined forces with Saint Peter's, our brother school, and we think the results will be most beneficial to all of us. The boys have volunteered to build the set and help out wherever we need them. Of course, they won't be involved in the play itself. This will be a first for us, but I'm sure we'll all take it in our stride. Are you wondering what I'm getting at?"

"Well, Sister, I'm a little mixed up."

"You needn't be. What you are going to do is write the play."

Collie let out a long low whoosh of air. "Really, Sister, thank you for thinking of me, but I couldn't. I mean, I just couldn't."

Sister sat back in her chair, rubbing the tips of her fingers together. "Aren't you feeling sorry about the poem you wrote, Colleen? Aren't you sitting before me wishing you had never done such a thing? I told you it isn't any good saying you're sorry. The Lord wants more than just a phrase."

"But I *am* sorry! I'll say a novena. I'll say ten. Or a rosary every morning for a year!"

The nun smiled for the first time. "I have already discussed this with the other sisters. We are all agreed. You will turn your talents to the happy disposal of the school. We are all confident you'll do a terrific job, Colleen."

"Really, Sister. I can't. I just can't. I never did anything like that before. Why can't we just get one of Shakespeare's or something?"

Sister Principal leaned forward again, still smiling. "You may return to your class, Colleen. Good morning."

"Good morning, Sister." Weakly, she rose and headed for the door.

"You have eight weeks," said the nun behind her as Collie breathed a secret prayer for the earth to open itself at her feet and swallow her whole. Writing a play for the school, the *whole school*, was absolutely out of the question. Absolutely.

Chapter sixteen

Like a dream the set went up, the lines were learned, the costumes made. There was no use trying to have classes: the whole school was carried away with last-minute preparations. The bishop was coming and they couldn't find a proper chair. The Most Reverend Mother was coming and nobody could remember if anyone had ordered flowers for her. The mayor was coming and he, a divorced man, was bringing a woman who wasn't his wife but one he intended to marry. They would expect to sit by the bishop of course, whatever in the world could be done? The piano sheets were missing. There was a hole in the curtain the size of a silver dollar but maybe no one would notice. Peculiar odors seeped through the walls from the chemistry lab: the audience would be forced to hold their noses or gag. Nuns fluttered about warning actresses to keep silent or their throats would spoil. Half-dazed actresses mumbling their parts tripped over each other in the hallways. The make-up coordinator experimented with shoeshine and dyed three girls pale green. The lighting coordinator blew a fuse. The flowers arrived and turned out to be deep yellow daffodils in a lily-of-the-valley spray. Someone remembered that the Most Reverend Mother thought daffodils were frivolous. Orchids were ordered. Although there was an outcry, it was decided that the mayor's lady would be presented the frivolity. The piano sheets were found. The fuse was fixed. The chemistry lab was disinfected. The hall smelled like a hospital ward and someone lit an incense stick. The hall smelled like burned raspberry tarts. The curtain was mended. Nothing could be done about the green girls but paint their faces with pancake-white and hope for the best. There remained a thousand things to be done. Where was Dutton? Nobody could find Dutton. An actress wanted a line changed because it was sticking in her throat like a sourball and she was in a panic. Where in the world was Dutton?

Huddled beneath a round writing table in the reference section of Our Lady of the Coronation Library, Collie was using the dictionary in her lap as a desk. Humming softly, she was writing as if her fingers were playing a familiar and beautiful tune.

James

she wrote; she sang.

James Patrick Rafferty
James
James
James

A delicious thought came in unannounced, and though the curl of the table legs pressed uncomfortably against her spine, she felt she was lying on goose-feather pillows. She uttered the sigh of a dreamer raptured by some impossibly happy dream.

> Mrs. James Patrick Rafferty
> Colleen Rafferty
> Colleen Elena Dutton Rafferty
> C. E. Rafferty, Wife of James

Like sugar to the lips, the thought could not pass without the most pleasant of sensations. She put down her pen. Love flooded her and flung her, head over heels, high above the mere ground. Love beat its wings against her rib cage. Love was the trampoline she walked on, the coach and six she rode like a lady in a fairy tale, the astonishingly splendid landscape she imagined, the face of James Patrick Rafferty as she first had seen him, bent over a stack of wood planks, wondering how he would unite them, for a platform was needed before the set could go up. James was wearing painters' overalls over his Saint Peter's blazer and tie, and though they were ragged with wear, there were fresh creases in the legs. James's overalls had a pocket for everything. There was a pocket for nails, a pocket for hammers, a pocket for pencils, a pocket for peppermint Life Savers, a place for everything and everything in its place. The other boys, the ordinary grimy boys, carried their things haphazardly, dropping here a tack, there a chewed-down ink pen, and all the while grunting like beasts in a barnyard. Above them James had soared. James had towered. James had straddled the whole of the world and looked radiantly down upon them.

"Where's the one that wrote the play?" James had asked of no one in particular. When Collie looked up from her notebook, he had turned on her two blue heavenly bodies of light, as he said, "How big you want this platform?"

He had stared into her eyes for such a long time she thought she might melt to the floor in a puddle. His gaze held her, transfixed her, sliced through her skin and bones to the very core of her heart and, once touching it, grasped and claimed it. Blood rushed to her head in a dizzying, throbbing rush. For an awful moment she'd felt as naked as if she'd just stepped out of the bathtub; in another instant her blood had drained, leaving chill and frost in her veins. All her senses had stood on end, tumbling one into the other. She saw him with her skin, smelled him with her ears, heard him with her eyes, and in a frenzy of confused excitement apprehended him in every pounding mesmerized part of her self.

"Ten by ten," she had somehow managed to answer, "with an eight-inch height. You'd better watch out for splinters," she added.

Then he smiled, a smile that spread over his face like sunlight breaking through fog. "Don't worry," he'd said, pulling sandpaper out of a pocket. His clear unswerving gaze told her that no matter what the problem he had a pocket to fix it.

"Oh by the way," he'd added, "I read your play. I found it while we were waiting for the wood. It's good. Real good. I never would've thought a girl could write so good. I just hope we can make a set good enough for it." His face had erupted in a grin. The white of his teeth had sparkled like stars. "I'm James. Want a Life Saver?"

Blood singing, Collie had accepted it as if it were a Host.

"There you are," clucked Sister Mary Librarian, yanking aside some chairs. "Heaven bless us, Colleen, the place has gone mad without you. I thought I might find you here. Work, work, work! Even the Maker had a rest! There's a girl, come along, they're needing you. Out of the books and into the world. The books'll wait but the world won't."

Collie looked up as though encountering something from another planet and hastily hid her papers. She followed the cheerful nun docilely, having only to breathe to see James's face.

"I didn't get a thing done all day, I'm so nervous," said Clare, wringing a dishtowel. "The phone didn't stop ringing once. I tell you, Colleen, the whole town's going up for the show. To think of it! School play at sixteen, Hollywood at thirty, that's what everyone's saying. Here, fill the water glasses for me, I'm in such a state I can't think. Let's see, the dresses are ironed, and Mary, I do wish you'd do something with your hair. Let me just stick a few pincurls in the front. You look like a lawnmower's been at you. For heaven's sake, Mary, don't look like that, one more look and your face'll stay that way forever. Then who'll marry you? Oh Martin, you're *not* going to wear that blue tie. Kangaroos are all right for the office, dear, but not your daughter's first play. Besides, the bishop'll be there. Oh Colleen, I wish you'd let us read it first! I do hope there's nothing bad in it, I'll never be able to hold up my head. Colleen, Colleen, are you listening to me? Colleen, you're awfully quiet!"

"It's nerves," said Martin.

"It's James," said Mary. "All she's thinking about these days is James. Goes around kissyface over that stupid James."

"Who?" said Martin, his eyebrows raised.

"Who?" echoed Clare eagerly.

"James, I said. He's the one that—"

Aghast that the name should fall so profanely from her sister's lips, Collie emptied the contents of the water pitcher on her sister's face. Ice cubes clattered to the table, the floor. Collie tore out of the kitchen, slamming the door behind her.

"Well!" exclaimed Martin rubbing the back of his head.

"Well!" echoed Clare, tossing Mary her towel. She sent her husband a triumphant look. "So it's a boy after all. I knew it must have been a boy! Go after her, Martin, and say she mustn't cry. If she cries her face'll be ruined. How'll it look for the author to show up at her own play with red eyes?"

"I'd like to make 'em black," grumbled a dripping Mary.

Slowly the hall filled. Parents greeted each other graciously, nervously rolling and unrolling the programs handed out by the white-gowned reception committee, all freshmen. Someone's grandfather stumbled and fell, taking with him half a row of empty seats. The bishop himself, personally excusing the old gentleman from injury, supervised things back into place. There were chuckles and handshakes all around. The Most Reverend Mother seized her orchids like a bride. The mayor boisterously pumped the bishop's arm. To everyone's horror, the mayor's lady flounced forward and bending as if to curtsy, planted a kiss on the bishop's ring. "She must be a Baptist," sighed Sister Mary Phillipa, Mistress Stage Manager, watching from a chink in the curtains. Sister Mary Agatha, Mistress of Ceremonies, quickly intervened and maneuvered the unfortunate lady's hands around the daffodils. She glowed, accepting them as if they were a prize at a spelling bee. "Girls, girls! Into place!" called Sister Manager. "It's show time!"

Scattering wildly, some thirty singers and dancers and musicians and dramatic speakers, each rouged and resolved and ready, assembled in the wings. Costumes were tucked in or puffed out. Hairdos were praised or were fussed over. Lines and snatches of songs were hastily murmured as currents of unbearable last-minute panic swept through the cast like electricity. Someone whispered she'd that moment forgotten her part. Someone else said she had a toothache. The girl singing the opening song said twenty frogs had just moved into her throat. "Quiet everyone, quiet!" ordered the very flushed Sister Manager. "And you," she added, cornering Collie, "you make scarce of yourself in the dressing room. We can't have you out in the audience. It's been my experience with playwrights that no sooner does the curtain go up than they're bolting for the girls' room with a sick stomach. Mind you, now!" Collie nodded blankly and remained stone still where she was. Sister Mary Librarian took her place hidden in the drapery folds, stage left, as prompter. Sister Mary Cecilia, guardian angel of the choir, took her place at the piano. Sister Mary Guidance, Mistress of Lighting, took her place at the switches. The lights dimmed. An expectant hush fell over the audience. Backstage the entire cast took a deep breath as Sister Manager's lips prayed a silent Hail Mary. The piano struck the opening notes of the school's traditional good-luck hymn, "Crowned Mother, Crowned Virgin, Take Thee Our Hearts."

"Amen," moved Sister Manager's lips, and everyone exhaled. "Break a leg, girls," she cheered.

Slowly, with a great rustling *whoosh*, the curtains parted.

"Get her out of there!"

Collie was standing in the middle of the stage like an old forgotten prop. Darting out of the way, she tripped over an entering actress and fell headlong into the lap of Sister Mary Librarian, who grabbed her by the shoulders and dumped her unceremoniously onto the landing outside stage left. Crossly, Sister closed the door on the playwright, leaving her wedged alone in the tight dark space.

Collie cursed the day she had ever thought of taking pen to paper. Miserably, utterly forgotten, she strained to hear what was going on onstage. The lines sounded strange and faraway. The very words she had made herself, out there on their own, had nothing in the world to do with her now. She plugged her ears with her fingers. She sucked on her teeth. She sat on her heels. She took off her shoes. She made loops and curls with their laces. She put them back on. She counted to one hundred and back. Surely Act One must be over.

But the thing had only reached page three. She groaned. Like Shakespeare, she had written five acts. Time had never seemed as long in rehearsal as it did in reality. I'll never make it, she thought grimly, tensing as the play reached a point where she'd scribbled "Audience Laughs" in the script.

The audience was not laughing. She chewed on her knuckles. She was done for. She would never write a single thing as long as she lived unless she went to work for a greeting card company. She would grow up to compose sorrowful rhymes for the insides of sympathy cards. That night, after the Finale, she would sneak out the back door, disguised in a nun's black shawl. Even her own mother wouldn't be able to recognize her. She would hitchhike a ride home. Maybe she would get lucky and be murdered. DUD PLAYWRIGHT BUTCHERED IN STOLEN FORD CONVERTIBLE, she imagined the headlines.

Suddenly a thunderous noise splattered the doors and the walls and the rafters. She covered her mouth to keep herself from yelping when she realized what it was.

"They love it!" cried Sister Manager at intermission.

The dressing room was crazy with whirling bodies, cascading dresses, squeals and laughter. Everyone was hugging. Someone handed Collie a grape juice bottle filled with champagne. She swallowed it all in a tingling gulp, gasped as some of it went in her nose. She sneezed once, twice, three times. Sister Manager said it looked like the playwright was coming down with a cold, and the girls all roared. In seconds the room took two steps to the right, then to the left, then settled into a pleasantly undulating rhythm. She grinned. Dimly she noticed her parents swim by. Clare was kissing everyone. Martin, in his kangaroo tie, was shaking hands. The bishop came in and drew a crucifix in the air to bless the rest of the play. A boy in a florist's cap appeared at the door with an armful of red roses. Sister Manager spied a dangling hem and rushed to repair it. Collie sank into a chair, exclaiming to herself what a very remarkable thing it was that nothing in the room was standing still. Someone tapped her shoulder. Out of a blur of black and white a face arose, the face of Sister Mary Anastasia.

"Congratulations, Colleen," she said, pressing her lips to Collie's very flushed cheek. "It's a wonderful play!"

"I'm lookin' fer Dutton. You Dutton?" The boy in the florist's cap edged past Sister Mary Anastasia and tugged at her arm. He was freckled and slightly cross-eyed. Collie was forced to blink several times to get his face into focus.

"I got flowers fer a Dutton. That you?"

She nodded, trying to make sense of the mysteriously floating vision of Sister Mary Anastasia, the freckles bopping about the strangely familiar florist's boy's face, the stunning red of the roses, the merry-go-round feel of the dressing room, the tart taste of the champagne, the throbbing deep inside she hoped was just her heart—and concluded that after all she must be asleep and dreaming.

"Watch out, she's going to be sick!" gasped Sister Manager. "Oh, I knew it!"

*　　*　　*

Act Three melted into Act Four. Act Four like a clock clicked into Act Five, and the audience, convinced that they'd got what they'd come for and more, leaped to their feet, applauding. "Author! Author!" they cried as the cast took bow after bow. "Author! Author!"

Skirts flying, Sister Manager raced down the hallway to fetch the playwright off the soothing cool unmoving bathroom floor. Collie with her roses was swept up to the stage. Blinking in the lights, she nodded like a sleepwalker, thinking only of the small white card in her hand that said,

Love,
James P. Rafferty

 1967

Chapter seventeen

Buds burst into bloom as she passed them by. Puppies strained at their leashes to lick her hands. She couldn't get over the amazing yellow way spring came into town, rolling itself out beneath furry white clouds that never in her life seemed thicker. The planet with all its countries, oceans, mountains, and time, was hers for one word: James. The sun rose in its honor, the moon shone to explain it, every star blinked its message across the night sky and she was the only one alive to understand it. Night after night she sat on the front porch with James, clasping hands, bending heads together over some funny thing James had just said.

> *Roses are red*
> *Leaves are green,*
> *The girl I love*
> *Is named Colleen*

composed James when he found out she liked poetry.

Goodnight, Colleen, goodnight,
I'll see you in my dreams!

said James every evening when Martin Dutton blinked the porch light and kept it blinking until she went in the house.

"You're not like the other girls, you know. You're special. You're not like the other girls at all. That's why I picked you to be my girl!" whispered James. His arms held her like a chair. Snuggling against his shoulder, playing with the soft dark hair that sprang in delicate angles out of the collar of James's shirt, Collie felt as though she were slipping into the warm deep reaches of a happiness she had never imagined possible. I'm James's girl! she said to the trees, the birds, her pillow. James's girl am I!

"Honestly, Colleen, don't you think you're seeing a bit too much of this boy?" said Clare, looking up over a bowl of plump ripe tomatoes. Meatballs were baking. Sausages fried. Chopping onions, Clare was crying.

She'll cry the day I marry, thought Collie. She'll tuck tissues in the bosom of her dress and cry right through my wedding.

Mother, she imagined herself saying, Mother, James has asked to take me for his bride. (Too stiff.)

Mother, I have something to tell you: James and I will marry. (Too bookish.)

Oh, by the way, Mother, did I mention that I'm going to marry James? (Too disrespectful.)

Oh Mother! I'm so happy! James wants to marry me! (Good.)

152

"I mean, he's taking up all your time, Colleen. What about writing another play? What about your friends at school? It seems to me that you're letting your school work go. You've been out with this boy every night. Really, Colleen, there's time enough. You're too young to . . ."

FAMOUS PLAYWRIGHT WEDS BRAIN SURGEON, she imagined.

FAMOUS PLAYWRIGHT WEDS RACING-CAR DRIVER.

FAMOUS PLAYWRIGHT WEDS SENATOR. (James was undecided.)

"Are you listening to me? Having a boyfriend to dance with at the dances is a nice thing for any girl. But you always were one to fly off to extremes, Colleen. Nobody knows that better than your own mother."

Collie looked up. Her mother's fingers were flying with expert grace through the tomatoes: slicing, chopping, stirring. Into her great pot went like witch's brew the onions, the garlic, the parsley, the meat. It was warm and comfortable in the kitchen. Life itself seemed to be bubbling.

What I ought to do, thought Collie as she imagined herself in an apron, cooking for James, humming as she went along, is ask her for her recipes.

"Mother . . ."

"And another thing, Colleen. I was talking with Sally Ferretini's mother the other day. You know Sally, that nice girl with the braids who goes to the public school. The one that almost drowned in the river last summer. What a fright that was! It seems Sally Ferretini used to go out with this James, and let me tell you what her mother said . . ."

Collie groaned. "No, Mother. Cut it out. I'm not going to sit here and listen to any stupid gossip of yours. When

I grow up and get married I'll *never* gossip. All anyone in this town can do is sit around and gossip."

She plugged her ears and began to slink off.

"Young lady! Young lady, you may think you're in love but let me tell you—oh!" exclaimed Clare as the supper began to boil over the top of the pot. "Oh, how I wish I had sons!"

"I heard that, Mother. I heard you say that and don't deny it." In her room, chin in hands, Collie stared out the window, thinking how one day she would have many sons. Women with daughters would be jealous and shower her with baby blankets and booties and tiny sweaters, all blue. In her own mind she imagined that it would be far nicer to have lots of daughters, who would grow up looking and acting like her, but that seemed wrong somehow. Selfish. When you had sons it was easier to hold up your head. Didn't everyone say so? To make everyone in town see what a good mother she could be, she would have ten sons, and name them in honor of Jesus's Apostles: Peter, Andrew, James Junior, John Patrick, Philip, Bartholomew, Thomas, Matthew, Jude and Baby Simon. Perhaps when that part was all finished and she had done her duty, she would have things her own way and have a baby girl. Even if her mother protested because it wasn't modest she would name her Baby Clare. Every one of the children would have James's smile, James's bottomless clear blue eyes, James's magnificent hands, twice the size of her own hands, hands that were as comfortable beneath the hood of a car as they were tapping out the beat of a song across her forehead. There was nothing James's hands could not do. When they closed around her wrists, hard and gentle at the same time, she'd say, Oh James, you have the hands of a musician. When they took a stuck eyelash out of her eye, she'd say, James, you have the hands of a surgeon. When they carved in a tree "James loves Colleen," she'd say they were artist's hands and cover them over and over with kisses as if they were baby kittens.

They claimed the town park for their own, nestling like spoons under elm trees whose old twisting roots opened their arms to give them room. They pitied everyone who wasn't in love. Are you sure you love me, Collie would say, are you absolutely sure? And hearing it once she must hear it again; she must hear it a thousand times. Like an abracadabra said over a hat the words were magic. Hold me, James, don't let go! He would wrap his arms around her and rock her like a boat. She would sail to the ends of the earth there, and ask once more if he truly did love her.

"Colleen," called her father from the living room, motioning a place beside him on the couch. She sat down, imagining him in a top hat and pleated formal coat, leading her down the aisle. His eyes were moist at the edges. No one in the standing-room-only church could believe what a splendid bride they were seeing. Her father was whispering how it seemed only yesterday that his little Colleen was asking how to pronounce long words in the newspaper: how quickly everything changes! At the steps of the altar stood James, nervously fingering the white flower in his buttonhole, every inch a man in overwhelming love with his bride-to-be. As the organ struck up "Here Comes the Bride," her father put down his newspaper. "Colleen, your mother and I spent half the afternoon with Sister Principal. I can't say that we're happy about what we heard."

Poor Sister Principal, she thought sadly. Imagine never falling in love! And breaking off at a gallop, her mind concocted an image of all the Coronation nuns sitting in a row at her wedding, weeping. They would be allowed to sit near the front, of course, to have a proper look. Poor things, never having a wedding of their own! She would remember to tell them not to bother with a wedding present; or if they insisted, she would donate half of whatever it was to charity.

"Colleen, whatever in the world is going on with your school work? Your grades were never a problem before."

"Oh, Dad, there's nothing wrong with my grades."

"The sisters are getting worried about you. It's not like you to let your work go. And what about the autumn skit you promised to write? Sister said you haven't started it."

"They wanted to have a silly little play for the new freshmen, Dad. It's too childish for me."

"Colleen, you're not acting like yourself at all. Sister says you're not paying attention to your classes."

Poor Dad, she thought. He doesn't have any idea what's really going on. Of course Sister is going to tell him terrible things. It's jealousy. Pure simple envy. Everyone knew she was James's girl. It was something every girl wanted to be. She, Colleen, who was, had to put up with the envy of everyone who wasn't. Even the sisters. She understood, though. She would do her best to behave charitably. The Christian thing to do would be for her to pretend it wasn't jealousy at all. Love has certainly made me a *good* person, she thought.

"I know that my teachers are only thinking of what's

best for me," she told her father. He patted her hand gently.

"That's right, Colleen. Now it's time for you to buckle down and get your work done. You never did have a problem with your classes and we don't want them to be a problem now. College isn't far off, you know."

"You're right, Dad. I'll catch up. I guess I slacked off a little bit, but I'll do my very best to get my grades up again."

"I was hoping you'd say that, Colleen."

The organ music swelled and resounded. The altar was covered with white lilies in silver-wrapped pots. All the lilies came from her mother's garden. Her dress twinkled with tiny diamonds. Its train stretched like clouds behind her, fourteen pews long. Mary was doing her best to hold it steady. As she approached James, he held out his hand. It quivered ever so slightly, not with nerves but with love. In his top hat, her father cleared his throat, a thing he always did when he didn't know what he ought to be saying. "Oh, Dad, you've been a wonderful father. Even though I'll be a wife now, I'll still be your daughter!"

In the pews the Coronation nuns wept with feeling.

"I was hoping you'd say that, Colleen," her father said as he turned her over to her beloved husband-to-be.

Clare silently withdrew a Kleenex from the top of her dress and pressed it to her eyes.

"I love you," said James in her ear, leading her to the priest.

* * *

Mary was sitting in the kitchen with a basketball, practicing her dribble. With ease she nudged the ball around each leg of the chair, under her knees, and up to her chin. Catching it neatly with one hand, she held it high over her head and set it spinning on the tips of her fingers.

"Bravo!" cried Collie in the doorway. She imagined that her sister was wearing, instead of gym shorts and a tattered t-shirt, a morning-sky-blue maid-of-honor floor-length dress with layers and layers of lace at the cuffs and shoulders. Mary's hat matched the dress. In the band of the hat were seven or eight fresh flowers, plucked from the bride's enormous bouquet. The bouquet had cost forty dollars. It had come all the way from Boston, a present from James.

When it comes time for the bride to toss her bouquet I'll make sure it's Mary who catches it, planned Collie. She saw herself alone on a small white balcony, anxiously looking down at the throng of wedding guests. Flashbulbs were popping like stars. Off to her right an orchestra was playing something quiet but cheerful. As she drew back her arm the music stopped. An excited hush shot through the crowd. As she brought her arm forward to throw her flowers, a drum rolled, louder and louder and louder—

"Hey, Coll! Come on outside and shoot some baskets with me," said Mary. "I need practice on my jump shots." Tucking the basketball under her arm, Mary ran her free hand through her short dark curly hair and flicked off the beads of sweat all over her forehead.

She's going to ruin my wedding, Collie thought. She'll sweat all over that beautiful dress: How will I ever be able to hold up my head?

Collie sank into a chair at the kitchen table, groaning into her hands.

"Aw, come on, Coll. Just for a little while. I'll shoot and you can guard."

Sudden pity splashed all over Collie. Poor Mary! Poor unwanted unhappy envious Mary. Nobody in the world was in love with Mary. Collie sighed. If she didn't have her as maid of honor, she would let Mary be something else.

"You coming?"

"Go on without me. I'll watch you from the window. Anyway, I can't play with you now. I'm waiting for James." Collie leaned back in the happy glow that came over her every time she said James's name. "He was supposed to be here about an hour ago, but his mother needed some help around the house. She's very fussy." Collie shrugged, rolling her eyes. Instead of saying "his mother" she had nearly said "my mother-in-law."

Mary's jaw dropped. "But I just saw James. Not twenty minutes ago when I was leaving field hockey practice at the gym. He was sitting on the gym steps with a bunch of his friends."

"That's impossible," said Collie. She saw at once that poor Mary was trying to hide her envy with a cruel and deliberate lie.

"I'm telling you what I saw!"

"It's no good, Mary. I can see right through your little game." Collie pushed herself away from the table and headed for the door.

Chapter eighteen

The Harvest Moon Hop was only a few hours away. Outside the Dutton house the trees knew it, and rippled a hundred shades of red in the slow evening breezes. Stray leaves came fluttering against her window as if they meant to come inside. Billowing on its hook, her dress was breathless with anticipation: a neck-to-toe swirl of taffeta and chiffon the colors of a lime sherbet cooler topped with shavings of lemon. When she tried it on it looked like something delicious being poured out of a frosty glass. Her mother had dyed a pair of new high-heeled shoes to match. Her father had surprised her with an evening bag that matched too, and dangled from her wrist like a lady's. The new white velvet evening gloves went up her arms past her elbows. Her hair was piled on top of her head in a gently curving upsweep with perfectly placed end-curls in the shape of ampersands. Tiny bows of green and yellow satin in alternating colors held all her hair in place. It felt like a very large and fragile paper hat. It had taken her mother all morning. With only an hour left, Clare was still fussing over the bows and curls like a restless artist in front of an easel.

"Watch what you're touching in those gloves," she warned. "Don't let them sag, Colleen. Pull them up and see you keep them there. A girl who lets her gloves sag is likely to do the same with her life. You want everything to be just right. I hear that all the sisters'll be wearing corsages that the priests at Saint Peter's bought. That's a nice touch. Mind you don't go touching anything greasy. That means car doors too. You never know what kind of grease packs up on car doors. Just you watch what you're touching!"

"They're not priests at Saint Peter's, Mother. They're brothers. Why do you have to call them priests when they're brothers?"

"It's the same thing, Colleen. And it's no good getting nervous. You just act like a lady and you'll have a good time at the dance. I remember how jittery I was, my first formal!"

Collie looked over her mother's shoulder into the mirror on her wall. From where she was standing it was impossible to see the top of her hair. The girl there looked back with a strange, pale expression, and Collie quickly turned away.

"Is she ready yet?" called Martin from downstairs.

"Hurry, Colleen, your father is waiting to take pictures. He wants to get a good shot of you coming down the stairs. Just like a princess!" Clare carefully took the dress down and held it out to her daughter. It was swishing like whispers.

"James'll be here any minute and he'll want you to be all ready. Colleen? Colleen, come away from that window! Do you want the neighbors to see the prom girl in her house-coat? Colleen, what's the matter with you? If you're worried about the dance, it's nothing new. Every girl is nervous when it's her first formal. Colleen, here's your dress. Colleen!"

At the bottom of the stairs Martin was humming the opening bars of the theme song to the Miss America pageant.

"I wish your Nana, God rest her soul, was here to see you in this dress. You'll be the prettiest girl there!" exclaimed Clare.

"Come on, Collie," called Mary. "The camera's ready!"

Collie took a deep breath, flexing herself like a diver poised at the edge of a jittery board. When she could trust herself to speak she turned to her mother.

"If you don't mind, I'd like to put it on myself. It's sort of special." She tried to smile. "Please. I just need one minute to myself, okay? You can wait downstairs and see me coming down."

Clare nodded with understanding and laid the dress across Collie's bed. She gave her a quick hug and left her alone. Collie closed the door behind her, listening. As soon as her mother was down the stairs, she quietly closed the latch and tried the door to make sure it was locked. She slipped out of her robe and into bluejeans and a sweater. There wasn't a thing to be done about her hair except wrap a scarf around it.

"Ten more minutes!" her father called impatiently.

She took a sealed envelope from under her pillow and slipped it under the door. Then she unlatched the window and crawled out onto the roof, easing herself down flat on her belly. It was a short jump to the sloping ground on the side of the house, and she landed in a pile of freshly raked leaves waiting for someone to set them on fire. Stealing around to the front, she saw her parents and her sister inside, standing near the window. Her father had his eye in the camera, ready to get her coming down the stairs like a princess. Her mother was wringing her hands nervously and looking upward.

"Come on, Collie," growled Mary.

"Go upstairs, Martin, and see what that girl is doing so long," said Clare. "James'll be here any minute. She's a nervous wreck."

Martin put down the camera and started climbing the stairs.

"I'd be nervous, too, if I was her," grumbled Mary. "It's probably those shoes. She's too chicken to walk in them 'cause she's scared of falling down. How's she gonna dance when she can't even walk?"

"Oh hush," said Clare, giving Mary a little push. "Your sister is a beautiful girl tonight. Don't you go doing anything to spoil it for her. Your turn'll come soon enough. Wipe that sulk off your face, young lady. You want to show your sister how pretty you think she looks."

Suddenly from the top of the stairs Martin gave a cry of surprise that sent Clare and Mary running.

Ducking low, Collie scooted out to the sidewalk and sprinted down the hill. The scarf around her head loosened as she ran. Green and yellow satin bows came undone, and left a jagged trail behind her.

"What are you *doing* out there? You scared me half to death!"

"Sh! Somebody might hear you. Open the window and let me in."

"Colleen, what in the world is going on? Look at you. Look at your hair! Why're you out of breath, did you run here? Will you answer me? Wait a minute, this is the Saint Peter's prom night. Colleen—"

"Never mind all that. Where are your parents?"

"In their room, watching television. Don't worry, they never come in here."

"Do you think you can borrow your father's car for a little while? Close your mouth, Ruthie. You look like you're seeing a ghost."

"I'm not going to do a single thing till you tell me what's going on."

"What's going on is an *emergency*, Ruthie. Are you going to help me or not?"

"Sit down for a minute and catch your breath. I'll go fix you some tea."

"*Ruthie!* Please! I hate tea. I don't want tea. I want you to borrow your father's car and drive me somewhere."

"How can I do that? You know what my father's like. He never lets me touch the car unless I'm on an errand. Anyway, I have a date. He'll be here in about ten minutes."

"What do you mean, you have a date?"

"His name is Roger. We're going steady. We always go out on Saturday nights. Maybe I could explain it to him, and you can come out with us tonight."

"Look, Ruthie, I came here because I thought you might help me. Forget it. I'll go find somebody else. If you'll get out of the way, I'll go out the way I came in."

"Wait. Wait a minute. Tell me what you have to do. If it won't take too long I'll say I have to go to the store or something."

"Say you ripped your stockings and you have to get another pair before what's-his-name gets here."

"Roger. His name is Roger."

"Okay. You get the car keys. I'll tell you everything in the car. Oh, Ruthie?"

"What?"

"Ruthie, I . . . I mean, this is real nice of you."

"That's okay."

"Ruthie, one more thing. Do you have any lipstick?"

"There's some in my handbag."

"Good. Don't forget your handbag. I'll meet you outside near the car. Whatever you do, don't say I'm here."

"Don't worry."

"Ruthie, one more thing: On your way out, will you take the telephone off the hook? Pretend it's an accident. My parents will probably be looking for me. I left in sort of a hurry. Go on, will you?"

Don't get upset or anything because I'm not here. I didn't go far, and I won't be long. I'm not going to the dance. I should have said so earlier today, but I couldn't. How could I, when everyone was making such a fuss? I'm not twelve years old. I can make up my own mind about important things. If you come out looking for me I will die of mortification. I'm sorry about the dress. Maybe we can save it for Mary, or return it to the store. Love and I'll see you soon, C.

"You're not making any sense, Colleen. You sneak in my window, make me come out here, and now you're not making sense. What do you mean, he attacked you? Why don't you talk in real talk?"

"Why don't you drive like you know what you're doing? For God's sake, Ruthie, you drive like a cow. We just missed that tree!"

"There's nothing wrong with how I drive. You stood him up, didn't you? Maybe we should drive by your house and see what's going on. James is probably standing on your front porch right now. With a corsage for you."

"Ruthie, if you drive anywhere *near* my street I'll jump out and die. You want a murder on your conscience?"

"Then tell me exactly what happened. From the beginning."

"Drive faster, Ruthie. You're going about eleven miles an hour."

"Tell me or I'll stop right now."

"Okay, okay." Casting about in her mind for the right words to tell the truth, she leaned back against the seat in Mr. Bent's big car. There came hulking like a half-remembered dream a peculiar memory of pain and confusion, and she wanted to shake her head violently from side to side to be rid of it. For the thousandth time that day she gritted her teeth and repeated to herself, *I won't cry. I won't, I won't, I won't.*

The car passed out of town and they cut open on the highway that led to Saint Peter's School, four blocks north of Coronation High. She imagined the way the road behind them was slowly filling with cars bearing her friends in evening costumes, each one tingling with the feel of adventure. She thought of her parents and her sister, fumbling at the door of her room. She thought of James, climbing the steps of the front porch, holding out the flowers he'd bought to match her dress. A picture of James's face floated by like a flashback in a movie, and instantly she was filled with the cold raw taste of anger, something that was large enough and powerful enough to hold on to.

"I hope his eyes fall out. I hope he rots in hell."

"I love you, Colleen. You're my girl and I love you," James had said. His breath was warm and soft in her ear, a tender tickling that spread in small flushes down her neck, over her breasts, which James was cupping in his hands as if they were two delicate and wonderful delights. Nothing in her life had ever prepared her for the way her body unfolded beneath James's hands. Every day she was Colleen the ordinary; every night she was James's girl. What had those two selves to do with each other? She woke up in the morning thinking of kissing James. She rushed to the supper table to get another meal out of the way to hurry and fly to James's arms. Her thrilling secret had nothing whatever to do with all the silly and senseless things she had to have done before she could be truly who she wanted to be: the girl James loved. Nothing seemed real except the way her body wanted to curl up under a tree beside James, the way her mouth wanted to kiss James's mouth again and again, the way the deepest, most secret and inner part of herself wanted to leap to the surface and be stroked, soothed, loved. Whenever she wrapped herself around James, a thousand things seemed to be happening all at once: she was warm and floating, she was sinking and safe, she was fierce and strong. The night before the Harvest Moon Hop, James wanted to know what color flowers he should bring. He was certain she would be the prettiest girl there. He wanted flowers to suit her. He was tickling the edges of her mouth with his tongue, and she was laughing. He didn't care what they cost. He would get whatever she wanted. She reached up to trace little circles around his neck, imagining herself with an armful of roses. A car passed by beyond the trees and a radio was playing. James was singing the words in her ear. She was laughing softly, loving the feel of having everything she wanted right there in her arms. But suddenly he wasn't singing anymore. Suddenly, as if she were skidding to the edge of something too frightening to look at, she felt herself tense and stiffen. The face that looked down upon her was James's, the face she loved, but something strange and scary had come into his eyes. His lips tightened across his bared teeth and he was breathing hard as his hands clamped down on hers, pinning her to the ground. For a moment she thought he was playing. "Cut it out," she said, trying to loosen his hold. But there wasn't anywhere to move to. His mouth closed on hers, hard and fast. His hands, rough and hostile now, seemed to be everywhere on her. His body was heavy and hard. Even as she struggled, he pressed her tightly, silently. Her scream caught at the back of her throat and seemed to lodge there, one more painful thing. He was saying something now, thickly, hoarsely. She relaxed, flattening herself, as if she were fighting with her sister and it was time to quit. He let go of one of her hands, muttering into her ear, but she couldn't make out what he was saying. She flexed her fingers, testing their strength, and, gathering herself, she drove her fist into the pit of his back and hammered as hard as she could. She'd caught him by surprise, and surprise made him reach back to stop her. In an instant she managed to break free. She scrambled to her feet, panting. There was a stone on the ground nearby and she scooped it up, holding it high, ready to fling it. James was kneeling near her feet, looking up with a curious smile.

"Don't. Wait. Colleen . . ." He rose, holding out his hand. She stepped backward. He ran his hands through his hair and rearranged his rumpled jacket. "Colleen, really, you shouldn't have done that." His voice was smooth, calm, as though he were talking to a small child who had misbehaved. "You shouldn't have let me do that, Colleen. I thought all this time you were a nice girl. What's the big idea anyway? You made me act like some kind of animal. I'm really surprised at you, Colleen."

Her jaw dropped in astonishment. He took a step closer, and she took another step away.

"I won't tell anyone about this if you won't." He took his

comb from his jacket and combed his hair. "Come on, I'll walk you home."

It was an old flat stone with dozens of tiny cracks. It fitted neatly into her palm. It was gray. Ordinary. She clenched it so tightly her knuckles whitened. She was shivering crazily. It was impossible to speak.

James zipped his jacket and turned his collar up. "It's late, Colleen. Are you coming now or aren't you?"

She felt numb. Her mind blanked, refusing to believe that the pain of a moment ago, the pain and the fear, had come from James. The stranger standing in front of her, holding out his hand, certainly couldn't have anything to do with the James she loved. She knew if she tried to talk she'd only start crying.

"If that's the way you want it, Colleen, I guess I'll just see you tomorrow night for the dance."

She shook her head, putting up a mighty struggle to hold back the tears.

"What do you mean, no? Aw, I'll forget this happened if you will. No grudges, okay? I'll pick you up around eight. Come on, Coll, don't just stand there like a statue. I won't tell anyone what you did. It'll be our secret, okay?" He held out his arms as if he meant to hug her, and for an awful moment she was sorely tempted to rush to him, hold him close, get back the warm gentle feel she had always felt there. The stone in her hand fell to the ground. Tears filled her eyes.

"You're still my girl, Coll."

The tears broke in a blinding, angry wave. She covered her face and turned away. When the crying stopped, she lifted her head, listening to his footsteps clap on the pavement through the park and disappear.

"How're we going to get in? Did you ever think of that?"

" 'Course I thought of that."

"I suppose you think we're going to march right in the front door past all those priests. This place is probably crawling with priests."

"They're not priests here, Ruthie. They're brothers. Drive around to the back; there's a parking lot there. Good, it doesn't look like anyone's here yet. Park over there near the door."

"C'mon, Colleen, we can't get in that way. It's got to be locked. They wouldn't expect anyone coming to the prom through the back door."

"Don't worry. It's open. The latch's been broken for years."

"How do you know?"

"I just know. What do you think, it's my first time coming to this place? That's the door we used every time there was a basketball game or something and—" She broke off quickly and fumbled with the handle of the car door. "Come on."

The door opened onto a long corridor where overhead pipes were hissing. They kept to the sides, walking on tiptoe, Collie leading the way. Below them came the sounds of a dance band tuning up, but otherwise it was silent in the gym. Collie stopped and turned around.

"This is the girls' room. Come on," she whispered.

"What if somebody's in there?"

"Then jump behind them and say boo!" She pushed the door open. "We don't have to turn on the lights. I can see it okay. There's the mirror. Keep the door open a crack in case anyone comes by. Now hand me the lipstick and stand by the door."

"What're you going to write, Colleen? Did you think of something? I can't see. What're you writing?"

"Sh-sh. What do you think? I'm writing the truth. James Rafferty is a rapist. A *rapist*. I'm putting the whole thing in big capital letters, for everyone to see."

"Wait a minute," said Ruthie. "Let's make it worse."

Collie took her hand away from the mirror and looked at Ruthanne with impatience. "Are you crazy? What worse thing can you possibly say about someone than *rapist*? You just keep watch, Ruthie. I'll take care of this."

But Ruthie shut the door and came into the restroom with an air of determination. "If you write that, people might just think it's someone being hysterical or something. What you want to do is make everyone stay away from him, don't you?"

In the darkness of the small bathroom, Collie felt herself staring hard at Ruthanne. She could not remember a single time Ruthanne had ever had an idea of her own. She toyed with the lipstick in her hand, trying to adjust her eyes to the darkness. "So what do I write?"

"I'm thinking."

Collie opened the door to let in a slant of light from the corridor. Caught in shadows, Ruthanne's face was screwed in thought. Her eyes were shut.

"It's getting late, for God's sake. We don't have any more time!" she whispered urgently. Ruthanne's eyes flashed open. To Collie's surprise, her eyes stayed in their places, two bright pools of light focusing on Collie with a singularly accurate aim. Collie felt an urge to cheer.

"I've got it!" Ruthanne seized the tube of lipstick and, as Collie stood open-mouthed in the doorway, she wrote in large block letters:

JAMES RAFFERTY HAS V.D. KEEP AWAY, IT'S INFECTIOUS.

Collie clasped her hands together and silently applauded. "It's perfect!"

Flushed and pleased, Ruthanne stepped back to admire the message. She dropped the lipstick back into her purse and said excitedly, "Let's go write it someplace else!"

Just then came sounds of footsteps near the boys' locker room at the other end of the hall. Collie felt her heart turn over.

"C'mon!" Collie grabbed Ruthanne's arm and they tore out the way they'd entered. Outside, cars were pulling into the driveway, headlights flashing. Collie kept her arms close to her head so that no one would recognize her, and when she made it back to the car, she slumped low in the seat. Ruthanne slid in beside her, eyes dancing. "Let's get out of here, Ruthie. Hurry up!"

She looked over her shoulder long enough to make out the long-gowned figures of girls on the arms of boys in suit coats, hurrying toward the brightly lit lights of Saint Peter's gym. She felt suddenly lighthearted, almost happy.

"Ruthie?"

"Colleen, if you're going to say one single word about

how I drive, I'm going to stop this car and throw you right out on the street."

"Okay. Okay, I won't." She leaned forward and snapped on the radio. Ruthanne giggled.

"You ought to see your hair, Colleen. It looks like a bunch of birds just flew out of it. Really, take a look for yourself." Ruthanne adjusted the rearview mirror, and Collie leaned herself toward it. Her hair was in shreds all over her face, tumbled and limp. All the bows were gone. But the eyes looking back were laughing. She was laughing so hard she didn't feel the tears running down the sides of her face and all over Mr. Bent's front seat.

When they pulled up outside the Dutton house the front porch light was on. She was mildly surprised to find there was nobody waiting there. She had half-expected a dozen police cruisers, sirens wailing.

Dear Ruthie,

There isn't any way I can pay you back except to let you know that any time you ever need somebody to be your friend, it's me. I hope Roger wasn't too mad at you for keeping him waiting. Anyway, you're worth waiting for, and you can tell him I said so.

It's been a week, and my parents are still walking around like I've got leprosy. They think I chickened out of the prom because I was afraid of going out of the house in a long gown. My father said if I was so worried I should have brought along a pair of sneakers to make me more comfortable. He said it wasn't the sort of thing I should go sneaking out of the house for. You know how my parents are. As soon as they'd found out I was gone they thought I must be lying in a gutter somewhere with my throat slit. When I got back they carried on like I was Lazarus. As soon as they got over it, my father went up and took the lock off my door. Now when I want privacy I have to push my bed against the door, and that stinks. All the same it was worth it. My mother cried and cried over the waste of my gown. She's awfully worried that I won't grow up right. Mary came and told me what had happened: "he" waited around for about an hour. Nobody had ever stood him up on a date and he couldn't figure out what to do. Mary says that while he was waiting he looked like he would have liked to put his fist through a wall or some-body's face. "He's really a creep," Mary said, and it was nice of her not to remind me of the time she tried warning me about him. I didn't tell Mary what he did to me. Some-day I might. Anyway, he left the house finally. Nobody knows where he went. I guess he must have figured out for himself that the last thing I wanted in the world was to be anywhere near him. Mary sat in the hallway the whole time he was waiting and didn't say a single word to him. "I don't talk to creeps," Mary said. Good old Mary. Remember in the old days when I wanted to sneak her into your bomb shelter so I could save her life? Well, I still do.

I hope you don't go out of your mind when I tell you the bad news. I almost didn't tell you so you could think our mission was successful. Well, you're not going to believe this, but nobody ever saw what we put on that mirror. Nobody. I should have planned it better. I guess they had a cleaning lady who went into the bathroom just before the prom started. Who would have thought of that?

Let's just hope that whoever that cleaning lady is, she has a big mouth.

When Monday came I went rushing to school, expecting everyone to tell me about the message on the mirror. That's how I figured it out about the cleaning lady: no one said a word. All they wanted to talk about was how I stood "him" up and why did I do such a thing, etc., etc. I said I never wanted to hear his name again as long as I live. Everyone got the idea that he's a creep. I say bad things about him every chance I get. I'll be shocked if any Coronation girl ever wants to be in the same room with him. I wish I'd thought of a cleaning lady, though. If I had, we could have put it in spray paint all over the gym walls. And in the parking lot. And all over town, on the railroad bridge and the sidewalks and every tree we came to.

One good thing did happen. He's not going out of his house very much. Everyone says he's afraid to show his face because he's so embarrassed that I stood him up.

I'm sorry I have to tell you that the plan failed. Afterward, I realized how much easier it would have been if I had gone to the police and had him arrested. Can that sort of thing be done, do you think?

I just wish I'd planned it better.

Anyway, what I want to say is thank you.

Guess I'll see you around.

Love,

Colleen

 1968

Chapter nineteen

"What I don't understand," said Clare, snapping thread off a spool with her teeth, "is why she has to pick a college halfway across the country when there's a perfectly good school not twenty miles away. You encouraged her, Martin. It's you who put these fool ideas in her head."

"I didn't have anything to do with it," said Martin, peering over the top of his new glasses. "The girl's got plenty ideas of her own. She doesn't need any help from me."

"Hrumf," she sniffed. "It's not right for an unmarried girl to go off so far from her mother."

"I think it's terrific," offered Mary, who was sitting at her parents' feet, busily rubbing liniment on her knees. "I think—"

"Nobody is asking you to think, young lady. Colleen! Colleen! Will you come down here! Bring the rest of those blouses. I want to get them all done. Colleen! Mary, go upstairs and tell that girl I want her down here. She's deaf, that's what she is."

"She's busy," said Mary. "She's got her door barricaded and she doesn't want anybody bothering her."

"Well, we'll just have to see about that." Clare put down her sewing and grumbled to the stairway. "I'm coming up, Colleen! I'm coming up and don't you go acting like you can't hear me. There's not even two days left and you haven't even started any packing. Do you hear me, Colleen?"

It had been coming for weeks, coming like a powerful and exciting thing, and even before she knew what it would turn out to be, she understood that it had to be right. It had to be real. Even before it had started forming itself into any words at all, it was meant to be something special. Starting with the same old flutter of her heart, the old familiar swishy feeling in her belly, the excitation fluttering at the edges of every waking moment and turning itself over in her dreams every night, it floated around trying to get itself said. The words came drifting in tiny pieces at first, unsure and skittish. Then she had to hold herself very still and swallow down the agony of not getting it right, of letting it make itself big enough inside her, of being patient enough to trust that sooner or later it would emerge, whatever it was. It ached for weeks. It dragged her down like a heavy weight, gnawing her, it seemed, right down to her bones. The first few times she thought it was ready, it wasn't, and went on cluttering her days and wrecking her sleep. Bothersome and irritating, it was determined to have its own way no matter what she did.

But when it came, it came suddenly and beautifully. It

rose out of her heart and it soared. She couldn't write fast enough to please it. She hardly knew what it was until it was over and she read it for herself. Her mother was thumping away at the door, but, first, there it was.

A Poem for Ruthanne

When we were girls the wintertime
shimmied up the black sides of trees
crazy with desire.
All night long the branches rattled the window like bones
as if it really might be worth it to put up a fight.
In the morning it was dazzling
it was dazzling and delicious
it was glinting and pitiless and giddy
with the cold we blew on our fingers:
two girls outside
where winter exploded and joy came.

When we were girls the wintertime
froze the river like a backbone,
the inky awkward troubled river froze
smooth as eyes
and there wasn't a thing alive to stop us
winging it bank to bank between the cries
that broke from our throats
whip-hard and thrilling. No wonder we loved the winter,
the hills we built and guarded
with our own two hands that the rest of the year
had to make do with smaller, more timid things.
Lady-things that the winter wouldn't have any part of.
We were invincible then.
We didn't care who it was
caught climbing up our hill.

We'd put out their eyes.
We'd knuckle-ball their teeth.
We'd cream 'em and if it ever came to that,
we'd kill.
On the way home we went the long way,
pausing in doorways, in and out of shadows,
linking hands to keep warm.

When we were girls the wintertime
lashed a fury across the sky
like a terrible child making messes.
Envious, we watched the winter
spin the wheels of our fathers' cars
deliriously on icy driveways
and it made our blood boil.
How we loved the winter!
the untidy thrill of the desolate
the clean and awesome look of a world
tipped upside down with disaster
and not a thing was moving but you and me.

When we were girls the wintertime
caught our laughter and flung it
over the back yards belly-deep in snow
over the trees where icicles dangled
over the rooftops where chimneys sputtered
thin white smoky puffs much, much smaller
than the breaths our own lips made.

When we were girls the wintertime
made us strong as steam engines.
We were giants.
We were like nothing else,
utterly indestructible.

"Colleen! Colleen Elena Dutton if you don't open this door right this minute I'm going to—I'm going to cancel the check I wrote for your tuition. Then see if you ever go away to college!"

She folded the poem and opened the suitcase waiting emptily on her bed. She tucked the poem into a side compartment and stuffed in a handful of socks and underwear, making sure that the poem was safely hidden. Someday she might show it to Clare. Someday she might show it to Ruthanne. Someday she might show it to the whole world. But for the moment, it was hers.

A strange, calm, deep feeling of pleasure came over her. Not since she was a very small child had she felt so utterly at home with herself. Part of her wanted to leap up in the air, shrieking for joy. Part of her wanted to curl up in a little ball and let the feeling of peace bubble about her, snug and warm and happy. Part of her paid attention to reality, which was that moment making a great deal of noise outside the room.

"Coming, Mother."

"I'm going to count to ten, Colleen. Enough is enough. One, two . . ."

She heaved the bed away from the door and shut the suitcase.

". . . three, four, five . . ."

She flung open the door and Clare came tumbling in sideways. Collie held out her arms and caught her neatly.

"Well!" exclaimed her mother, out of breath. "And what have you been doing in here all day? I sent you up here to pack." Clare looked about the room as if she expected to

122008

J
C
Cooney, Ellen.
 Small-town girl.

find something awful hiding in the corners. Still holding on, Collie gave her mother a squeeze. For the first time in her life she realized that she could put her arms around Clare's shoulders without having to stand on tiptoe. Her mother seemed to notice the same thing, and quickly looked away. She eyed the suitcase suspiciously.

"You'd better be all packed, young lady. You better not be dawdling. It's nearly time." Her eyes went liquidy and she bit her lip, folding her arms across her chest. She sniffed softly.

Back came Collie's arms around her mother's shoulders. "Don't worry, Mother," she said soothingly. "I've been doing just what I'm supposed to."

122008

DATE DUE